Introduction

As our Father does his works in our lives, he graciously intersects our path with the many he has prepared in advance to help us. While *Life, Love and Leading* has been a work in process for nearly 20 years, its preparation has spanned my lifetime and required the faithful input of hundreds.

What follows is the *Leading* section. *Leading* applies the foundational aspects described in the *Life* section of who God is and what he requires of us - *collectively* - that we might better synergize our organizations.

Flourishing organizations utilize system and structure that align with that of Adonai as *he* administers *his* kingdom - on earth as it is in heaven. Collectively discerned and highly productive relationally, organizations of any kind and size are led by the power of the Holy Spirit, consistent with the teachings of Jesus, as the Father within us does his works. Not making of us robots, we become willing participants in creative collaboration - *collectively* - growing hearts after God as the *Family* of God doing the *will* of God.

Acts 13:22
And when he had removed him (Saul), he raised up David to be their king, of whom he testified and said, 'I have found in David the son of Jesse <u>*a man after my heart, who will do all my will.'*</u>

The world is continually telling us that we must think and logic and work our way through to each decision. The equivalent of leaning on our own understanding:

Proverbs 3:3-8
5 <u>*Trust in the Lord with all your heart, and do not lean on your own understanding (mind)*</u>*. 6 In all your ways acknowledge him, and he will make straight your paths. 7* <u>*Be not wise in your own eyes (mind)*</u>*; fear the Lord, and turn away from evil. 8 It will be healing to your flesh and refreshment to your bones.*

The wisdom that follows does not so much come from me, but from a lifetime of collaborating with God and the many wise counselors he has put in my path. Proverbs 11:14 tells us that where there is no guidance the people fall, but in an abundance of counselors there is victory. May it be so for you.

Preface

If you think you are a good leader, prove it by not using Hierarchy & Authority. Then you'll know. The best of leaders don't need it. I've seen it over and over again.

When originally submitted to the publishing arm of a large Christian leadership consulting organization, I was told that *Leading* is badly needed for all leaders, church leaders especially, and should be a required textbook in every seminary and bible college. They wondered aloud, however, how many would be open to it – since most are so deeply oriented to hierarchical management. That conversation brought about the writing of the supportive preparatory *Life* and *Love* sections that you have hopefully read prior to now beginning *Leading*. *Leading* was re-written to follow these sections, and an understanding of their content must be assumed to avoid duplication.

Though described foundationally in *Life*, as we proceed in *Leading* we will build upon the criticality of eliminating the Authority bias from our operating systems and structures. When we organize and operate in the foundational understanding of the ways God has for us, we will only need him and the leadings Adonai provides his disciples *together* – that none should perish.

When we use Authority, Unity and the collective Wisdom offered to us by God are not our number one priority.

As described in great detail in *Life*, the Hebrew word *talmid* translated for us to English is disciple. The plural is *talmidim*. Unlike disciple or student or apprentice which suggest a learning, doing and practical application process, *talmid* describes a *becoming* process. Talmidim desire to *become* just like their rabbi. It is more than the practical application of the knowledge we gain. It is more than taking actions based upon our understanding of his teachings. A talmid of Jesus will not use hierarchical authority or control to accomplish *their* will. Rather, in the *collective wisdom* God provides us all, we will only say and do what the Father gives us to say and do. *Just like Jesus*. In the *collective wisdom* God provides, we will see our divided churches, families and nation be restored – *as rivers of living water flood out of us collectively* – one with him.

Leading

Uniting God's People to *More* Productive Service

From the book

Life, Love & Leading

Leading

All scripture is English Standard Version (ESV) unless otherwise indicated.

Leading

As with *Life* and *Love*, the use of capital letters to personify the various characteristics and behaviors of God and his Enemies continues here.

Chapter One

Who Will Reverse The Trend?

These are exciting days. Though for years and years we've been closing a net of eight churches every day here in the USA, we are now clearly at the dawn of a new awakening of God's people.

Over the last 20-30 years, the internet has made it possible for thousands of Christian scholars to peer review each other's work from anywhere in the world. Most importantly, this has led to their ability to collaborate, confirm, and identify original scriptural context that has been lost down through the ages. As we saw in the *Life* portion of our series *Life, Love and Leading*, this lost context is essential to our depth of understanding and therefore to whether or not we will succeed in making disciples.

Having been able to regain these cultural contexts of what Jesus was saying to the people of Jesus' day, we are now radically reforming our understanding of how we lead "church" and our errant way of trying to make disciples of all nations.

Primary among these concepts is our lost understanding of the Hebrew word *talmid* – from which our word disciple was translated. As was stated in great detail in the *Life* portion of *Life, Love and Leading*, we have our understanding of this word all wrong – and it changes *everything*!

A talmid is probably different than you think because we do not have any word for it in our English language. Unlike the words disciple or student or apprentice that suggest a learning and doing process, the word talmid is a Hebrew term that describes a becoming process. Talmidim desire to become just like their rabbi. It is more than the practical application of the knowledge gained. It is more than taking actions based upon our understanding of his teachings. A talmid of Rabbi Jesus will have a heart after the Father, be growing to reflect the very character of Jesus and be gaining the mind and attitudes of Christ.

Primary to the concept of being a talmid of Rabbi Jesus, one who is *becoming* more and more like him, is the fact that Jesus only ever said and did what the Father gave him to say and do. We will, too, as we remember that he said his sheep know his voice and follow; and unless we come as a child we will never enter the kingdom of heaven.

As described in great scriptural detail in *Life*, becoming like Jesus:

- *I only say and do what the Father gives me to say and do.*
- *I see what the Father is doing and behave likewise.*
- *I do nothing of my own accord.*
- *I do as the Father commands, that the world may know I love the Father.*
- *Unless I come as a child, I will never enter the Kingdom of heaven.*
- *My sheep know my voice and they follow.*
- *...for apart from me you can do nothing.*
- *Blessed are you when you walk in my attitudes.*

Further, as was elaborated upon in *Life*, the foundational attitudes of Jesus are listed in the Matthew 5 portion of the Sermon on the Mount that we call the Beatitudes. These are truly the attitudes that Jesus continually walked around in, and are those that we, too, are to more and more be walking around in as we *become* more and more like him.

Walking continually in Jesus' attitudes, we will more and more be predisposed to responding to those in the world around us with language and actions that produce good fruit - fruit of the Spirit.

As we discard our worldly hierarchical ways of authority and the world's *manipulate to control* strategies - learned from childhood on - our Jesus attitudes will reduce conflict, disarm a portion of our aggressors and model for them the well-lived life – a life pleasing to God. Then, as God has displayed for us from the very beginning, we will let them choose for themselves how they will live – though the consequences be eternal.

To continue on in the hierarchical ways of the world, we must dismiss what God said to Samuel when they said they wanted a king over them; and what Jesus said to his talmidim when they were told that there must not be any use of hierarchy among them. Though having a king over them *became* expedient in MANagement, what they actually gave themselves over to was being controlled by people rather than being *collectively led* by God.

1 Samuel 8:7-9

7 And the Lord said to Samuel, "Obey the voice of the people in all that they say to you, for they have not rejected you, but they have rejected me from being king over them. 8 According to all the deeds that they have done, from the day I brought them up out of Egypt even to this day, forsaking me and serving other gods, so they are also doing to you. 9 Now then, obey their voice; only you shall solemnly warn them and show them the ways of the king who shall reign over them."

Luke 22:24-27

24 A dispute also arose among them, as to which of them was to be regarded as the greatest. 25 And he said to them, "The kings of the Gentiles exercise lordship over them, and those in authority over them are called benefactors. 26 But not so with you. Rather, let the greatest among you become as the youngest, and the leader as one who serves. 27 For who is the greater, one who reclines at table or one who serves? Is it not the one who reclines at table? But I am among you as the one who serves.

Mark 9:33-35

33 And they came to Capernaum. And when he was in the house he asked them, "What were you discussing on the way?" 34 But they kept silent, for on the way they had argued with one another about who was the greatest. 35 And he sat down and called the twelve. And he said to them, "If anyone would be first, he must be last of all and servant of all."

Mark 10:42-45

42 And Jesus called them to him and said to them, "You know that those who are considered rulers of the Gentiles lord it over them, and their great ones exercise authority over them. 43 But it shall not be so among you. But whoever would be great among you must be your servant, 44 and whoever would be first among you must be slave of all. 45 For even the Son of Man came not to be served but to serve, and to give his life as a ransom for many."

Colossians 2:8

See to it that no one takes you captive by philosophy and empty deceit, according to human tradition (Authority), according to the elemental spirits of the world (the World OS), and not according to Christ.

John 17:20-23

"... may they all be one, just as you, Father, are in me, and I in you, that they also may be in us, ... that they may be one even as we are one,

I in them and you in me, that they may become perfectly one, so that the world may know that you sent me ... "

1 Corinthians 11:3a
But I want you to understand that the head of every man is Christ

Ephesians 1:22
And he put all things under his feet and gave him as head over all things to the church,

As they walked with Jesus, the talmidim's argument over who was greatest among them could only have been important in the determination of who had the most power, and therefore the ability to use it. They were trying to determine the hierarchy of *who had Authority over whom.*

1 Thessalonians 5:12-13
12 We ask you, brothers, to respect those who labor among you and are (watching) over you in the Lord and admonish you, 13 and to esteem them very highly in love because of their work. Be at peace among yourselves.

Taken out of context, leaders have used the selective reading of 1 Thessalonians 5:12 above *to take Authority over congregants* in the Lord. As we have seen in *Life*, the totality of scripture in context does not agree with their assertion. As was identified in great detail in *Life*, it is simply a tradition of mankind that we prefer, so that we may better Control the people around us.

Scripture identifies that Christ is the Head, our only authority, and he gives us leadership roles that collectively facilitate Wisdom in choosing – producing good fruit and Unity among his people. As you will see, even the international consultants for large Fortune 500 multi-national corporations have come around to abandoning authoritarian models based upon the military chain of command and are instead teaching the use of God's Unity Operating System. They have been proving that God's way works best. It's clear, the use of Authority is out! Relational *collective* Wisdom is *in*!

Unity At All Costs: Co-Leadership

Over the last 50 years, international corporate consultants and psychologists have been proving God's Unity Operating System and Structure most effective. Case study upon case study exist, we need only translate the results.

Kate Ludeman and Eddie Erlandson are co-developers of the Alpha Assessment, used by over 18,000 high-capacity leaders in 45 countries. Globally recognized consultants, executive coaches, speakers and authors – they work with the CEOs of some of the world's largest corporations to improve their approach to change management, innovation, risk-taking, board communications and alignment (alignment = Unity).

They bring a unique approach to coaching analytical, data-oriented CEOs who want to expand their emotional intelligence but who do not fully value some of the softer leadership capabilities (tending toward a productivity versus relational preference). They show executives the impact of their leadership on performance and motivate teams to break through their tendencies to rationalize problems - and therefore adhere to the status quo. Their insights transform average executive teams into highly effective teams where major problems are openly vetted (transparency), problems are fully owned (repentance), and productive debate (iron sharpening iron) leads to alignment (Unity) and Mutual Accountability (all of the information from all of the people).

The international consultants for Fortune 500 multi-national corporations have come around to abandoning authoritarian models based upon the military chain of command and are instead teaching the use of God's Unity Operating System. They have been proving that God's way works best. It's clear, the use of Authority is out! Relational collective Wisdom is in!

In their work the authors show alphas how to leverage their unique strengths while confronting their destructive flip side risks. To paraphrase, they describe the need for balanced complementary Co-Leadership by passion-aligned but diversely gifted individuals, and describe the inability of any CEO to survive long term without such an appropriate partnership.

They describe the inability of any CEO to survive long term without such an appropriate partnership.

****

We are no better than ancient Israel. We use phrases like, "Time is of the essence!" to justify authoritarian individual decisive action. It sure is expedient, isn't it? With one person in Authority as the Boss/Sr. Pastor/CEO/President/Chairman, answers can be given and decisions made quickly! "Something must be done! Lead, follow or get out of the way!" Though the resulting relational damage decimates Unity in relationships, families, organizations and nations.

Clearly, Division from and Hierarchy over, is not the culture God desires for us. These cause conflict, loss of relationship, disunity and poorer decisions through singularity. The sins of the parents have been being passed down to the third and fourth generation for generations. For generations of generations, and this has been happening for thousands of years. It has become so deeply ingrained in our ***Man***agement Culture that we rarely imagine there could be any other way.

We've carried on with it for thousands of years because we think it works! It's expeditious! Who has time to sit around trying to build consensus when we could be *getting things done*?!!! (My way!)

Synergy finds its foundation in the organizational climate.
As long as our seminaries and Bible colleges teach organization under the hierarchical military chain of command, we will be unable to synergistically operate our churches in Unity - in God's Unity Operating System – with us as body parts and Christ the only Head.

There is a way to operate *everything* in God's Unity Operating System. I have seen it work in businesses, churches and non-profits - as have other consultants and authors. Jesus' attitudes (the Beatitudes) promise blessing upon those who walk in his attitudes as his talmidim, and through the *rivers* of living water that shall flow from each one of us to others. Collectively, combined, it looks to me like our churches should *collectively* be causing a combined *flood* of living water to flow out to those in our communities! Is it true and occurring for you, your church and your community?

****

The Role Of The Rabbi In Jesus' Day

In consideration of our ways, his ways and the ways of the world, consider that the original followers of the resurrected Jesus were called followers of ***The*** Way. The Way ***he*** lived. The Way ***he*** loved. The Way ***he*** served. The role of the rabbi in Jesus' day was to teach the people ***how*** to fulfill the Torah. That is to say, to teach the people ***how*** to live a life pleasing to God. Jesus' Way simplified the totality of the scripture so as to help the people avoid an imbalance toward the Law and their minds. He helped them to understand that *a balance of their heart, soul and mind was necessary for the living of a life pleasing to God.*

The Way trained *talmidim* who *became* like him more and more - not disciples, or students or apprentices who learned *what* he taught and then *applied it* to their own lives as they saw fit. No. Jesus' Way was to point out *how* the world was living according to *its own* way of thinking. Small "g" gods unto themselves, *thinking* their way through to their *own* decisions on *how to live.*

****

As we saw in Life, as a talmid, I am becoming more and more like Jesus:

- *I only say and do what the Father gives me to say and do.*
- *I see what the Father is doing and behave likewise.*
- *I do nothing of my own accord.*
- *I do as the Father commands, that the world may know I love the Father.*
- *Unless I come as a child, I will never enter the Kingdom of heaven.*
- *My sheep know my voice and they follow.*
- *...for apart from Him I can do nothing.*
- *I am blessed when I walk in His attitudes.*

Unfortunately, these core culturally Hebrew understandings were left behind in Israel as we left for the other cultures of the world. The first European cultures filtered the text of the Bible into their own hierarchical Hellenistic cultural context, and we therefore lost so very much of its meaning. Originally called followers of The Way, that is, followers of Jesus who taught us the way to live a life pleasing to God, we have since become 250 doctrinal divisions, leaning on our own understandings and following them.

As was detailed and described throughout the *Life* book, true talmidim of Rabbi Jesus will evidence Jesus' attitudes – producing fruit of the Spirit just like their Rabbi Jesus:

True talmidim will evidence:

- Dominion over the earth, but not over people. (Genesis 1:26-30)
  - Give us a king. (1 Samuel 8:4-22)
  - Jesus said it shall not be so among you. (Mark 10:42-45)
- The Ten Commandments (Exodus 20:3-17)
- Love the Lord your God with all your heart, soul, mind and strength, your neighbor as yourself and one another as I have loved you. (Mark 12:30-31, John 13:34-35)
- "Love" active in service. (John 12:26, Mark 9:35, Mark 10:45, Galatians 5:13, Matthew 20:26-27, 1 Samuel 12:24)
- Hearts after the Father in attitudes consistent with the Beatitudes: Jesus' attitudes. (Matthew 5:2-12)
- Fruit of the Spirit language and actions. (Galatians 5:22-24)
- The Unity, character and attributes of John 17.
- Knowing God's voice and be following *Him*. (John 10:27)
- Creative collaboration and participation in accomplishing the will of the Father. (Genesis 2:19-20, 1 Kings 22:19-23, Mark 6:34-44)
- Only saying and doing what the Father gives them to say and do. (John 5:19, John 12:49-50, John 14:10)
- The elimination of Anger, Judgement, Condemnation, Hierarchy and Manipulate To Control behaviors from their lives. (Romans 1:28-32, Colossians 3:1-17, Galatians 5:13-26, John 17)
- The overcoming of the temptations and desires of the flesh, their sacrifice nothing compared to Jesus' sacrifice on our behalf. (Romans 1:18-32, Colossians 3:1-17, Galatians 5:13-26, Leviticus 18, Ephesians 5:1-21, James 4:1-12, 1 Peter 2:11-12, Ephesians 2:1-7, 1 John 2:3-6)
- That they are *becoming* mature and effective laborers more and more: the 12, the 70 and the 500.

Having been able to regain these culturally Hebrew contexts of what Jesus was saying to the people of Jesus' day, we are now radically reforming our understanding of "church" and our *errant* ways of trying to make disciples of all nations.

Over the last 20 years, I've been following much of this and recently noticed that it's being accepted by the seminaries of repute in our day. Since our scholars have found agreement, it's time for our seminaries, pastors, and families to be awakened to the fact that church decline has been occurring precisely because of the absence of such critically essential biblical context. This is foundational information upon which I believe all of the more than 250 denominations of the Christian church in the USA will agree.

Chapter Two

Unite Your People To *More* Productive Service

"To manipulate, drive or manage people is not the same thing as to lead them. The sheepdog forcibly maneuvers the sheep, whereas the biblical shepherd simply calls as he calmly walks ahead of the sheep. This distinction between the sheepdog and the shepherd is profoundly significant for how we think of our work as leaders of Christ's people. We must ask ourselves frequently which role we are fulfilling and constantly return ourselves, if necessary, to the practice of the shepherd."
Dallas Willard, "Hearing God," p. 81

MANipulate, Drive, MANage, MANeuver: Man's ways! Not God's!
Large multi-national corporations utilizing the World Operating System have been going the way of the Unity Operating System through Unified Co-Leadership for a number of decades now. Leaders are giving up their hierarchical models based upon the Military Chain Of Command and are instead synergizing into Teams of Groups and Groups of Teams to be more accountable and sustainable in productivity *relationally*. The traditional Authoritarian system and structure that seemed to make so much sense to us inherently led to conflict, division and periods of lost productivity.

Flatter organizational structures are more sustainably productive. Co-Leadership in God's Unity Operating System, compared to leadership in hierarchical models, is like the classic story of the *Tortoise and the Hare*, with the Hare's many unproductive rabbit trails. Slow and steady really does win the race, Unity really is sustainable. His yoke really is easy and his burden really is light when our productivity comes according to God's Direction, pace and timing – not ours.

In the Authoritarian system and structure, when our lead leader roared our lambs submitted and the other lions around him gradually decided to leave or just leave him alone. Without other strong high-capacity lions around to challenge his thinking and strengthen our collective DNA, we emboldened his Individuated Authoritarian Leadership – allowing more and more conflict to remain between us. Given the loss of our synergistic high-capacity lions, he and his rubber stamps made poorer decisions that eventually led to his demise. Since the whole process typically takes many years, once the lead lion was gone there were few high-capacity lions left within. A classic Bell Curve, our story was the living out of a roller coaster ride that led us back to where we started – searching for Unity, trying to develop productive relationships and hoping that Peace that surpasses all understanding might prevail as we look again to God - for the rebuilding of organizations of all types.

Psalm 127:1-2

1 Unless the Lord builds the house, those who build it labor in vain. Unless the Lord watches over the city, the watchman stays awake in vain. 2 It is in vain that you rise up early and go late to rest, eating the bread of anxious toil; for he gives to his beloved sleep.

Putting the bad experience behind us, our tendencies were to hire someone more relational to take his place, but that was never as productive as when we had the lion leading! Where is the balance? It comes with Co-Leadership from both!

Co-Leadership instead searches for all of the strong high-capacity leaders it can find and invites them into highly productive relational Co-Leadership opportunities where *iron may sharpen iron* in Unity. Top-down models prop up our leaders, send them into hiding and cause reduced transparency throughout the organization. Co-Leadership uses Mutual Accountability as opposed to Authority and helps our leaders remain humble productively.

Proverbs 27:17

Iron sharpens iron, and one man sharpens another.

Knowing that the best of us will fail when using the world's Hierarchical/Authority based operating system, Co-Leaders replace it with God's Unity Operating System & Structure for The Whole Body. Submitting to God as the only Authority, they constantly refer to a set of Unity values that allow all of The Body to be *connected with every supporting ligament, Christ as the Head.* The Authoritarian model has winners and losers and the Teacher/Student (or Teacher/Disciple) model frequently leads to Teacher Followers in Leadership Replication. But the Unity Operating System develops and sustains Unity throughout The Body as we collectively discern the mind of Christ as his *talmidim.* Spirit led, he turbo-charges our efforts and scales them up - *collectively.*

****

In Jesus' day, the role of the rabbi was to "teach the people *how* to fulfill the Torah". That is to say, *how* to live a life pleasing to God. Spending every minute of every day with their rabbi, *talmidim* would watch and see and hear and learn *how* he helped people understand and fulfill the Torah. Both by his words and by his actions.

But what are talmidim? Talmidim are what we in the USA erroneously call disciples, students and apprentices:

As described in detail in Life and Gravitas, a talmid is probably different than you think because we do not have any word for it in our English language. The English word translated for us from Hebrew is disciple. Unlike the words disciple or student or apprentice that suggest a learning and doing process to us, the word talmid is a Hebrew term that describes a becoming process. Talmidim desire to become just like their rabbi. It is more than the practical application of the knowledge we gain. It is more than taking actions based upon our understanding of his teachings. It was not just to know what the rabbi knew, but to be what the rabbi was. A talmid of Rabbi Jesus desires to become just like him, and to live as he lived. Making more and more talmidim!

As was also described in depth in *Life* and *Gravitas*, if *we* will endeavor to *become* like Jesus, the making of talmidim will require *individual* conversational time in ongoing *life-on-life* discussion. Not forsaking the fellowship, a talmid will also be associated with some sort of *group* of talmidim - continually discussing *how to become more and more like Jesus*. Not only that, but *how to help others understand what it means* to live a life pleasing to God in *their* becoming.

When Jesus said go and make talmidim of all nations, that did not mean "Just go teach people (disciples, students, apprentices) the Bible.". He said, "Go help people become like me, teaching them all I have commanded you!"

****

In organizations of all kinds, development following his Unity Operating System and Structure considers the need for *talmidim* and a wholistically complete view. The Authoritarian system and structure consistently evolves over time to exclude critical high-capacity leadership Body Parts, resulting in the loss of full function and a dependence upon inflated payroll budgets. Patterned into Groups of Teams and Teams of Groups, his Unity system and structure utilizes a full complement of high-capacity leadership giftedness such that the Spirit may turbo-charge synergism.

Using the 12 Teams I propose, we are better able to remain United and provide *facilitative vision across all Teams* for synergized collaboration and better communication. Using it, EVERY team, department or ministry you can imagine will fit within one of the 12 Teams and every potential employee, minister or congregant will have a better chance of finding their connection to satisfying service. If we will think of Wholeness from the beginning, we will be preparing the Whole Body with *collective* eyes that see and ears that hear.

Authority based models subtly squelch those who would disagree with us. Co-Leadership invites all of the information into decision making for the development of broad mutually supportive service. How does it work without Authority? Why does it work? How do Co-Leaders lead? Why doesn't it fail?

Highly impactful Co-Leadership in God's Unity Operating System includes a shared understanding of individual and team giftedness as well as openness about our destructive flipside tendencies. Co-Leadership with the expectation of Mutually Accountable participation allows *all* of the parts of The Body to weigh in on every issue so that all of the information needed for good decision-making may be sincerely offered, requested and heard. Co-Leadership in Teams of Groups and Groups of Teams is transparent so that other strong high-capacity leaders may identify their synergistic complementary fit. *Man*agement in the opaque is just a method for keeping them out of the loop and out of our hair.

God and his Unity Operating System do not hide behind policy and Authoritarian posturing. His is accountable and does not fear the litigious. His is an anomaly to which people run. It leads to ongoing One-ness, better decisions, excellence and Sigmoid Curves.

If churches and Non-Profit/NGOs will use it to Unite *across* our communities *for* our communities, we will also need a Whole Body Structure. This *Leading* section shares my best understanding of the comprehensive System and Structure upon which God has consistently helped us flourish with a minimum of conflict – though *iron sharpens iron*. It is totally scalable and incredibly inclusive.

****

In my career of leadership, development, consulting and mentoring, I have generally found it to be true that people, when confronted with a problem, tend to want to look at that problem from where they sit in the moment as opposed to its beginning – the foundation that allowed it to develop in the first place. The tendency we all have is to look back a few steps to see how it is that we arrived where we are and then try to back up to that point and start over, but that rarely works for the biggest of issues. I have found that where we *think* it started is rarely correct – problems typically spring from our *Operating System and Organizational Structure*. To be sure, the root of the problem requires some digging.

Our tendencies become more and more automatic as we age. For the most part, these tendencies are the foundation upon which we build our relationships, and it is this very foundation that sets up most of our *relational* and *operational* problems. This was described in great detail in the *Life* section.

I need to monitor me, my reputation with others and how it is that they have arrived at their conclusions. The World Operating System clouds our judgement when we do this. The Unity Operating System opens our hearts and minds for our great mutual benefit. As described in detail in *Life*, God's fruit of the Spirit ways (Galatians 5:22-23) lead us to language and actions in humility and with the attitudes of the Beatitudes: Jesus' attitudes (Matthew 5:2-12). These lead us to say and to do in ways consistent with his character, that give us a reputation for walking in his will, that bring Peace that surpasses all understanding, and a quiet confidence borne of him.

The World Operating System utilizes Authority in the hierarchical Military Chain Of Command. The Unity Operating System is led by Adonai alone, the end result being accomplishment of the Father's will through the broad giftedness and collective wisdom given to *all* as *willing participants* in *creative collaboration*.

We need to be introspective, holding deeper discussions with ourselves and others, while inquiring of the Father all along the way, that he might do his works in us and help us learn from our past.

****

While the things that we know so very well are what we lean upon to bring us success, the things that we do not know very well continually trip us up and curtail that success. I've found these same issues everywhere I've been. No person, culture, country, church or business can avoid the glass ceiling of ignorance: the hole in our knowledge.

We all tend to customize our operating system to make it fit our personal belief system – for most of us it is a form of the Parallels Operating System described in Chapter Seven of the *Life* section. Over time we create a culture upon *that* operating system that *becomes* specific to us – and this leads us in the direction of making gods of ourselves.

Now is a good time to stop and take a look at yourself and your organization. Does your operating system and organizational structure assume Hierarchy and Authority? Or collective wisdom, collaborative leadership and Unity based decision-making without the use of "expedient voting"? More than likely, it is sometimes one and sometimes the other – as in the Parallels OS we discussed in *Life*.

What formed your *Individual* Culture? Was it your Family Culture? Your Church Culture? Your School Culture? Your Boss' Culture? Pop Culture? By what criteria do you make decisions? All of these "Cultures" influenced you in that. But more than any other, the Military Chain Of Command Culture has had the greatest impact on the way you think and the decisions you feel comfortable making. As was also described in detail in the *Life* section, the Military Chain Of Command Culture has been deeply ingrained in us with ongoing reinforcement for thousands of years.

"That's just the way it is.
Some things will never change!
That's just the way it is...
Awwww, but don't you believe them!"
Bruce Hornsby, The Way It Is, 1986

To overcome our past World OS and structure programming, the best next step is all the way back to where our organization first started. This sometimes takes a lot of leg work, but usually not. If we instead "jump back" to the beginning of the entity to see the operating system and structure under which it was organized, we will often quickly find that our original assumptions were at fault.

These foundational beliefs were the basis for every decision made afterwards.

Operating in Unity

Tremendous insights are available for the benefit of leaders and teams who will spend time together in the interest of more cohesive function. There is no better time to utilize this than at the inception of every team, business, organization or entity. In this way, as new team members are considered, they may be apprised of the unique way they will need to operate if they are to join us. It is also much easier to reference these conversations later if and when behavioral issues occur.

If we have agreed to use fruit of the Spirit language in the attitudes of the Beatitudes while also utilizing the insights of the behavioral sciences - we will be able to remind them that this was described from the beginning and is why these Values hang on our walls for ongoing reference as well.

As described in detail in Chapter Five of the *Love* section, recent advances in the science of personality bring greater clarity to our roles as "triune imagers" (We will build upon that Chapter Five description here in Chapters Three through Seven as we proceed.). Personality assessments and the associated characterizations of our tendencies illuminate for us the great complementary value of differences on our teams. Individuals find the detailed information available in personality characterizations instructive for the development of relational interactions in any environment. Equipped with a better understanding of personal tendencies, it is far easier for us to take positions of grace, rather than ones of posturing so as to avoid that which is uncomfortable or unfamiliar. Grounded by an abiding value that broad team diversity is highly beneficial, we make better decisions as we seek out those whose perspectives are different than our own. Strengthened by the wisdom gained, polarizing Fundamental Attribution Errors may be avoided at home, work and play.

Fundamental Attribution Errors occur when we jump to conclusions about a person's *motivation* to behave in an observable way. FAEs block Unity as we attribute ill intentions to another's behavior – thereby helping us to rationalize conflict avoidance strategies. The synergistic potential between complementary personalities is often scuttled by this deception, causing synergistically diverse Body Parts to reject Connectivity.

In his book, The Advantage, Pat Lencione describes a Fundamental Attribution Error incident and then goes on to explain them this way:

> Fundamental Attribution Errors are a fascinating phenomenon that prevent people who don't know one another well from building trust. As sophisticated and complex as it may sound, it's really quite simple.
>
> At the heart of the fundamental attribution error is the tendency of human beings to attribute the negative or frustrating behavior of their colleagues to their intentions and personalities - while attributing their own negative or frustrating behavior to environmental factors. If I see a dad at the grocery store scowling at his 5-year-old daughter and wagging his finger in her face, I'm likely to conclude that the guy has an anger problem and needs some counseling. If I find myself scowling and wagging my finger in the face of my own five-year-old, I'm likely to conclude that my behavior is caused by my unruly child or that I'm just having a tough day.
>
> Of course this kind of misattribution, where we give ourselves the benefit of the doubt, but assume the worst about others, breaks down trust on a team. The best way to combat it is to help team members understand one another on a fundamental level and to give them as much information as possible about who a person is and why this person might act the way that he or she does. By doing this, we greatly increase the likelihood that people will replace their unfair judgments with insight and empathy, qualities that allow a team to build trust and goodwill with one another. Or as the Prayer of St. Francis goes, we must seek to understand more than to be understood. Though that is not always the case, *the benefits of greater understanding can sometimes be staggering and immediate*.

He goes on to share another transformative example of a leader jumping to a conclusion as to another's motivation and later states: *The only way for teams to build real trust is for team members to come clean about who they are, warts and all.*

When our leaders choose minimal transparency, we all suffer! We have all been unfairly Judged by people who seem to want to take us down, but so too it was for Jesus. Why should it be any different for us?

More importantly, as was developed in *Life* and *Love*, we are far more effective in these interactions with hearts after the Father, humbly postured in the attitudes of the Beatitudes, and shared in fruit of the Spirit language and actions.

In defensive posture, the World Operating System encourages partial truths protectively through policy statements and hierarchical rationalizations. Over time the sharing of partial truth becomes easier and easier. Over time, more and more is done behind closed doors where potential embarrassments precipitate further defensive rationalizations toward translucency and the opaque. Over time, without transparency we do not hear needed correction - the very voices God is sending for our benefit!

When our *Fundamental Attribution Errors* conclude a given person's motivation, we have eyes that do not see and ears that do not hear. FAEs work like a tool to make things personal, support syllogism and help us justify our ways. We often use syllogism and FAEs to maintain control over direction:

A syllogism (an inferred conclusion) is a kind of logical argument that applies deductive reasoning to arrive at a conclusion based on two or more premises that are asserted or assumed to be true.

However, when one premise is the requirement for Hierarchy and Authority, every conclusion that follows will be at least partially false. As we act upon these subtly false deductions, our own subsequent behaviors may be more easily rationalized - the honest result of believing the Enemy's foundational Authority Deception.

Chapter Three

Team Transparency Facilitates Team Strength

Meyers Briggs: Over the last 20-25 years, refinements to the prior understandings of the Meyers-Briggs Type Indicator have led to a far more detailed understanding of the tendencies of each type. Having evolved over many decades, the MBTI identifies 4 quadrants of Types with 4 variations each for a total of 16 basic types. Over the decades, the 4 types in the quadrants have been given a myriad of poorly descriptive sets of names that bring little benefit to individual understanding. For example, identifying people as Sanguines, Cholerics, Melancholics and Phlegmatics these days requires us to pull out a dictionary for assistance. The current state of refinements now avail very clear understandings that are surprisingly accurate. It is far more helpful as well to use these more accurate descriptors of Idealist, Guardian, Artisan and Rational, though in my experience the older less valuable information is more often used.

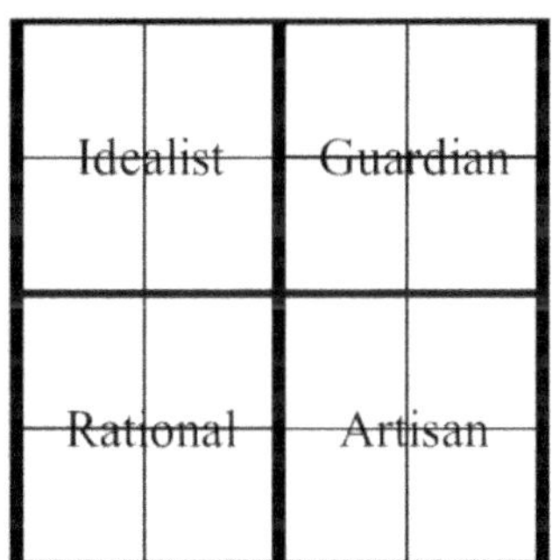

In their book *Working Together*, Isachsen and Berens detail each of the 16 types with 10-15 pages (each!) of significantly valuable information regarding Leadership Style, Values, Attitude, Skills, Driving Force, Energy Direction, Authority Orientation, Role Perception, Conflict Resolution, Modes of Learning and Blind Spots & Pitfalls.

DiSC: Applications for the DiSC assessment are similar to the MBTI, however, there are very significant differences as well. While each contain 4 quadrants of Types, the DiSC assessment identifies 3 variations each for a total of 12 basic types. The 4 types in the DiSC quadrants are: Dominance, Influence, Steadiness and Conscientiousness.

This assessment tool also yields surprising accuracy for those who answer honestly. Inscape Publishing has several inexpensive assessments available for individuals and groups seeking to better understand their interpersonal relationships. As with the MBTI, but differently, tremendous insights are available for the strengthening of team Unity and synergies.

The outside expertise to facilitate MBTI and DiSC for us exists in every community, and quite often inexpensively so.

Maturity, Education, Experience: As we look at the various types of giftedness that assist us in understanding the complexity of people, we cannot ignore the infinite variability between individual maturity, education and experience. Each are impacted by our initial nature/nurture environment, as well as that of our parents since each had their own. All of these are impacted by economic status, geography, faith, educational availability, local culture, outside mentoring, world view influences, etc.

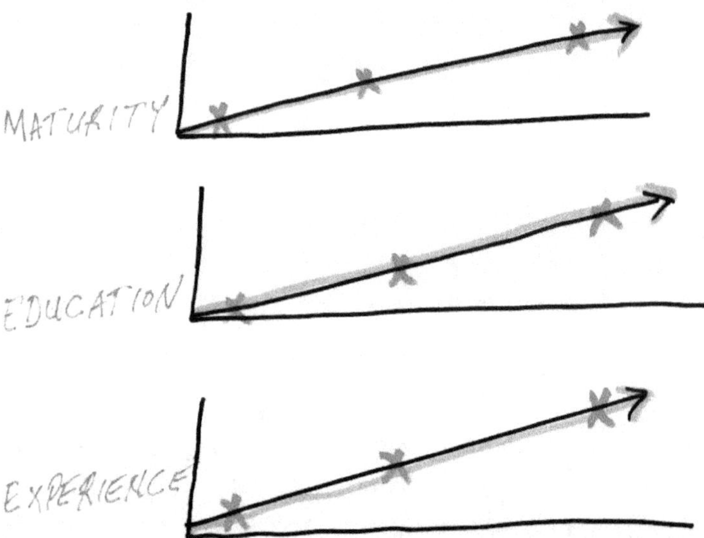

God has gifted us all in unique and diverse ways. In Genesis we learn that we have been made in God's triune image. In *Love*, we described how we may plausibly describe our triune roles as "imagers" in terms of Directors,

Reconcilers and Active Implementers (We will build upon *Love's* Chapter Five description here in Chapters Three through Seven as we proceed.).

The Book of Samuel and those describing the Old Testament prophets and kings teach us that we are not designed to lead alone. Jesus confirmed that when he told us that we are not the One in Authority. When he came, he re-established his Unity Operating System with his talmidim, that all would discern collectively and follow in the *Father's* will.

Luke 22:24-27

24 A dispute also arose among them, as to which of them was to be regarded as the greatest. 25 And he said to them, "The kings of the Gentiles exercise lordship over them, and those in authority over them are called benefactors. 26 But not so with you. Rather, let the greatest among you become as the youngest, and the leader as one who serves. 27 For who is the greater, one who reclines at table or one who serves? Is it not the one who reclines at table? But I am among you as the one who serves.

Who was greatest among them could only have been important in the determination of who had the most power, and therefore the ability to use it. They were trying to determine the hierarchy of *who had Authority over whom.*

Mark 9:33-35

33 And they came to Capernaum. And when he was in the house he asked them, "What were you discussing on the way?" 34 But they kept silent, for on the way they had argued with one another about who was the greatest. 35 And he sat down and called the twelve. And he said to them, "If anyone would be first, he must be last of all and servant of all."

Mark 10:42-45

42 And Jesus called them to him and said to them, "You know that those who are considered rulers of the Gentiles lord it over them, and their great ones exercise authority over them. 43 But it shall not be so among you. But whoever would be great among you must be your servant, 44 and whoever would be first among you must be slave of all. 45 For even the Son of Man came not to be served but to serve, and to give his life as a ransom for many."

Colossians 2:8

See to it that no one takes you captive by philosophy and empty deceit, according to human tradition (Authority), according to the elemental spirits of the world (the hierarchical World OS), and not according to Christ.

John 17:20-23

"... may they all be one, just as you, Father, are in me, and I in you, that they also may be in us, ... that they may be one even as we are one, I in them and you in me, that they may become perfectly one, so that the world may know that you sent me ..."

1 Corinthians 11:3a

But I want you to understand that the head of every man is Christ

Ephesians 1:22

And he put all things under his feet and gave him as head over all things to the church,

Several decades after Jesus rose from the dead and ascended into heaven, unbelieving Israel, retaining its corrupt Authoritarian power, was decimated.

Proverbs 29:18

Where there is no prophetic vision the people cast off restraint, but blessed is he who keeps the law.

Proverbs 29:18 NIV

Where there is no revelation, people cast off restraint; but blessed is the one who heeds wisdom's instruction.

Be aware! We use phrases like, "Time is of the essence!" to justify Authoritarian individual decisive action. With one person in Authority as the Boss/Sr. Pastor/CEO/President/Chairman, answers can be given and decisions made quickly. "Something must be done! Lead, follow or get out of the way!" Though the resulting relational damage decimates Unity in relationships, families, organizations and nations.

Synergy finds its foundation in the organizational climate. As long as our businesses, seminaries and bible colleges teach organization under the military chain of command, we will be unable to synergistically operate our churches and businesses in Unity - in God's Unity Operating System and Structure - with us as body parts and Christ the only Head.

There is a way to operate *everything* in The Unity Operating System and Structure. I have seen it work in businesses, churches and non-profits - as have other consultants and authors. God is blessing those of us in these churches, businesses and organizations as we operate currently, and will also bless those who are operating in them, *in him, at the end of our finite period of offering* (Described in *Life* as the end of our earthly life, our only opportunity to choose to Accept, follow and thereby gain life with Adonai for all eternity).

****

The New Testament reveals that we receive gifts from the Spirit. Science has helped us further understand our Director, Reconciler and Active Implementer portions with MBTI, DiSC, StrengthsFinder, Alpha Assessments and others. While there are only two basic types of leaders (*Directors* and *Reconcilers*), personality science has clarified the tremendous diversity of leadership giftedness within these two types - as well as their destructive flip side tendencies (as described in depth in *Life* and *Love*).

We are not neat little classifications on a chart. The most basic of calculations when combining each of the above factors results in a minimum of 5 million possible combinations - each one a part of The Body. If we will then consider the infinite amount of gradations between each type's linear extrapolations, we can easily agree that the individuality of Body Parts is infinite. Therefore, we cannot know where to place a Part. God tells the Part where it fits, though we may be helpful in pointing a direction.

The uninformed among us use impressions, perceptions, our differences, syllogism, FAEs and our previous experiences to get a feel for people and whether or not they fit. We are not allowed that luxury since *all* have a fit somewhere, even if as leaders we may sometimes need to Kindly and Gently use *fruit of the Spirit language* to facilitate Connection somewhere else!

In relational interaction, and especially upon subjects in which we differ, feelings and impressions are frequently Fundamental Attribution Errors that facilitate exclusion and only partial Body development. Whether a church, business or organization of any kind, the Enemy uses these against us as we select for people who are more like us than not. The end result being that we tend to exclude the very Parts of The Body that God has sent us for *wholeness* and *the transforming and renewal of our minds, that none should perish.* As we will see, FAEs cause Leader *Replication* as opposed to Leader *Multiplication*, the evolution of which weakens our effectiveness and shortens our tenure.

Leader Replication weakens our effectiveness and shortens our tenure.

We are highly specialized individuals. He told us so. Each of us have been designed for a purpose. Each have specific labors of love laid out for us that will help others in their area of need. Each are needed to show them the love of God within us and, perhaps little by little, help them to come to know and love him, too. Who we are meant to *become* cannot be known with any certainty, but these assessment tools and an understanding of ourselves in an Adonai-ically Triune way help us to better know what we are to be about.

None of us can tell *you* what to do either. We may help you to understand you and tell you what we see in you, but he is the One telling you always. He is sometimes whispering it and sometimes shouting it. "I have placed your passion within you. That for which your heart burns is my desire for you. I have gifted you to be a part of the whole solution - not the whole part, but your part - in concert and in synergy with all of the other parts. They need your Co-Labor-ation, too!"

When we realize just how powerfully we fit together for synergistic productivity in true Unity, we may just take the time to communicate Fundamental Attribution concerns so as to help each other with our fit. Arms and feet do not fit together, and they should not try! But that doesn't mean that we cannot help those parts find their fit on the same Body serving in differing ways. Our Adversary teaches us to disrespect those who are different, but that is not God's way.

Where passions align, differing giftedness is needed
to better accomplish the service.

Hands and feet *work* together, but they don't *fit* together. People passionate for the swift movement of feet don't *fit* with people passionate for the deft machinations of the fingers of the hand, but they are all parts of the same Body. We must understand and value our differences so that The Body may be Complete, Connected and fully functioning according to the design of our Creator.

When people of differing skill sets align themselves with people of the same passionate interest, they tend to be energized by working together. A sense of accomplishment, a renewed belief in what could be and a greater confidence to continue is instilled as they synergistically apply their combined skill sets to their endeavor of import.

****

Regarding churches, while small groups of people gathering to increase their knowledge through bible study, sermon application and such is necessary, why are we so lop-sided in doing so? These groups may be effective for a season of time, but they typically fizzle out if there is not also a passion-aligned service component. Otherwise, we are like the university student who never graduates and goes to work, but instead remains on campus for more learning. Life-long-learning is a good thing, but Wisdom is only gained through the practical application *of* that learning. Graduation into service is a necessary component!

Serving groups Unite diversely gifted people into an aligned area of passionate service as well as study, such that they may grow in Christ together for decades. Joyful service is the Christ-tie that binds them together, their diversity adding richness to the fabric of their lives as they also serve each other.

Look around at your community of churches. It is my guess that you see Body Parts everywhere with few "supporting ligaments". Reconcilers have been trying to facilitate Connectedness between churches for decades. Now, in over 150 cities across our nation, there is a new Connectedness evolving into community-wide collaborative service. If we will be successful at the community scale, we had better be working on it in our churches.

Isaiah 43:19
Behold, I am doing a new thing; now it springs forth,
do you not perceive it?

Chapter Four

Leader Multiplication, Not Leader Replication

When we use Authority, Unity and the collective Wisdom offered to us by God are not our number one priority.

- He wants us to be One with him and says that we are all parts of his Body of One, Christ as the Head.
- He is scalable. He scales his Unity *down* to you and me individually and *up* to be able to include every one of the people in the world – at the same time!
- His DNA of Unity is unchanged at any scale. Made in his image, our "DNA of Unity" is corrupted or otherwise damaged whenever we utilize Authority.
- He has no different amount of conflict or division or disunity at the individual level than he does at scale. He simply has none.
- Anything that is of him will look like him at any scale. Anything less than pure has been <u>*man*aged and *man*euvered and is being *man*ipulated by us</u>. Our abounding impurities in the Authoritarian World Operating System cause ongoing pain and retribution, but in his Unity Operating System and Structure for us, grace is sufficient when we fail.

We were taught to ask that his kingdom come and his will be done on earth as it is in heaven. We therefore have no excuse for rationalizing that growing in Kingdom Unity is not possible among us as long as we are on this earth. On the other hand, it is *definitely* not possible in the World Operating System.

As leaders, we do not honor God when we leverage our leadership giftedness and vision to overstep our bounds. No leader should be exempt from testing. Directors and Reconcilers need Active Implementers to Gently and Patiently Persevere with Kindness to point out leader hypocrisy and error without fear of Retribution. Active Implementers need to "esteem leaders because of their work", but not glorify or enable bad behavior.

Some use the following as a proof text to take Authority over people, but that is not what the totality of scripture is saying. This portion is talking about the care that leaders are to take as they *keep watch* and Gently speak God's wisdom into our lives:

1 Thessalonians 5:12-22
12 We ask you, brothers, to respect those who labor among you and are (watching) over you in the Lord and admonish you, 13 and to esteem them very highly in love because of their work. Be at peace among yourselves. 14 And we urge you, brothers, admonish the idle, encourage the fainthearted, help the weak, be patient with them all. 15 See that no one repays anyone evil for evil, but always seek to do good to one another and to everyone. 16 Rejoice always, 17 pray without ceasing, 18 give thanks in all circumstances; for this is the will of God in Christ Jesus for you. 19 Do not quench the Spirit. 20 Do not despise prophecies, 21 but test everything; hold fast what is good. 22 Abstain from every form of evil.

Disunity is difficult for leaders to overcome because we are its willing collaborators in the Authoritarian world system. It's a lot easier to get your way if you can describe an Our Way versus Their Way of thinking – and can out-vote the opposing view (Politics grow Division!). Still others describe votes of Unity and the Wisdom of consensus but do not understand that their results are due to the elimination of opposing views during Leader Replication. As Pat Lencione describes in his book The Advantage, we need to have all of the information from all of the people if we hope to be Unified in Truly Wise decisions together.

Unity At All Costs: Co-Leadership
Over the last 50 years, international corporate consultants and psychologists have been proving God's Unity Operating System and Structure most effective. Case study upon case study exist, we need only translate the results.

Kate Ludeman and Eddie Erlandson are co-developers of the Alpha Assessment, used by over 18,000 high-capacity leaders in 45 countries. Globally recognized consultants, executive coaches, speakers and authors – they work with the CEOs of some of the world's largest corporations to improve their approach to change management, innovation, risk-taking, board communications and alignment (alignment = Unity).

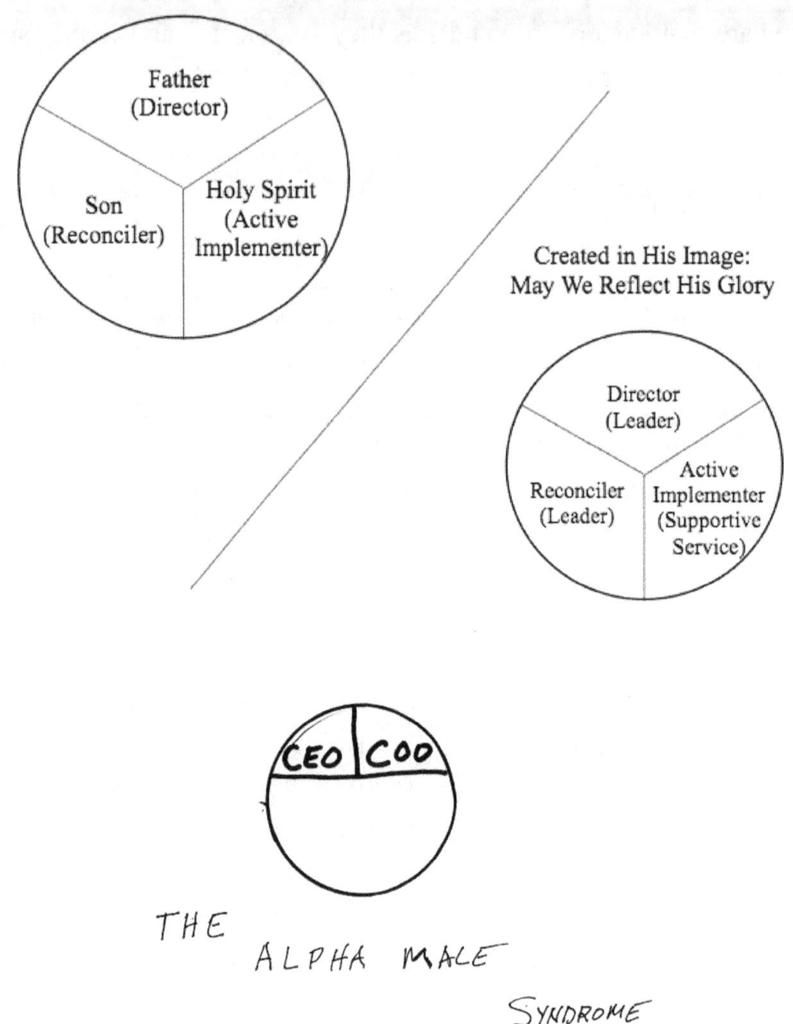

They bring a unique approach to coaching analytical, data-oriented CEOs who want to expand their emotional intelligence but who do not fully value some of the softer leadership capabilities (tending toward a productivity versus relational preference). They show executives the impact of their leadership on performance and motivate teams to break through their tendencies to rationalize problems, and therefore adhere to the status quo. Their insights transform average executive teams into highly effective teams where major problems are openly vetted (transparency), problems are fully owned (repentance), and productive debate (iron sharpening iron) leads to alignment (Unity) and Mutual Accountability (all of the information from all of the people).

One of the greatest confirmations I derived from their book *The Alpha Male Syndrome* is their description of the CEO (Chief Executive Officer) / COO (Chief Operating Officer) relationship. Their PhD and MD training, personality centered insights and decades of large corporate coaching and consultative expertise led them to assimilate multiples of correlating personality data as it related to the performance of CEO/COO teams.

While women tend to be put off by *The Alpha Male Syndrome* book title, the term is simply an animal kingdom analogy for passionate high-capacity leaders of all genders who tend to utilize the power of Hierarchy and Authority when asserting their will. This most often brings to mind the image of the lion, the king of the jungle, but is just as true for female alphas everywhere!

In their work the authors show alphas how to leverage their unique strengths while confronting their destructive flip side risks. To paraphrase, they describe the need for balanced complementary Co-Leadership by passion-aligned but diversely gifted individuals, and describe the inability of any CEO to survive long term without such an appropriate partnership.

They describe the inability of any CEO to survive long term without such an appropriate partnership.

Like MBTI and DiSC, they too identify 4 types. But unlike MBTI and DiSC that are applicable across all people groups, The Alpha Assessment has been prepared with only high-capacity leaders – *leaders of leaders* - in mind. The 4 types of high-capacity leaders they identify are: Commander, Visionary, Strategist and Executor – and they very strongly correlate to MBTI and DiSC. Another exception is that it is possible for a person to have giftedness for up to three of the four types.

While Commanders might also be Visionaries and/or Strategists, they cannot also be Executors. Similarly, while Executors might also be Visionaries and/or Strategists, they cannot be Commanders. Commanders need Executors and vice versa - Co-Leadership.

Commanders tend to be confident with a drive toward productivity. Their tendency is toward Command and Control, and if without Reconciler maturity, they tend to appear arrogant, pushy and somewhat heartless.

Executors tend to continually seek to understand the human side of the situation as it evolves. Their tendency is toward harmonious relationships, and if without Director maturity, tend to spend too much time in dialogue trying to build consensus at the expense of productivity.

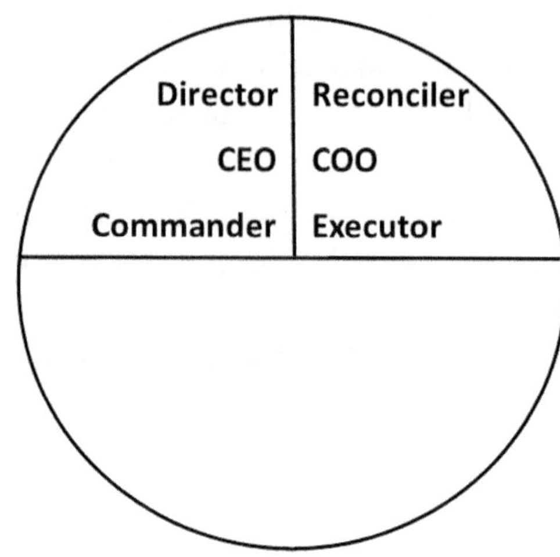

Generally, we may say that Directors tend to be Commanders and that Reconcilers tend to be Executors, but hopefully we are each endeavoring toward a mature balance in our Director/Reconciler selves. If we will allow the sanctification of the Holy Spirit to occur through our Co-Leadership experiences and the Mutual Accountability feed-back offered by those around us, God will little by little and more and more (2 Corinthians 3:18, Romans 8:29) produce a balanced maturity in us - the evidence of which is good fruit, fruit of the Spirit. We otherwise risk our Adversary's exploitation of our weakness in any given situation.

****

During planning, it is very likely that Director-CEO-Commanders and Reconciler-COO-Executors – who probably share overlapping Visionary and Strategist giftedness – will come up with a balanced plan together. Given their complementary giftedness and ability to articulate their views, their plan will likely be quite comprehensive.

It tends to go bad, however, if the CEO and COO are *both* Director-Commanders. Though the two may start off with similar passion and in alignment on the plan, eventually they will diverge and develop a rift in their relationship. Small departures in convictions on the best way forward may lead to great rifts in relationship as time goes by. And if that is not enough, Director-*COO*-Commanders also tend to command *what* they want *when* they want. If the Director-CEO-Commander arrives for a look-see with the

Director-<u>*COO*</u>-Commander, they run the risk of a very public exchange on the matter.

Unfortunately, Director-CEO-Commanders tend to place indebted young Director-Commanders alongside themselves in the COO position. In this way, they believe, they will gain greater productivity with little risk of losing Control. After all, the indebted young Director-<u>*COO*</u>-Commander will find it hard to risk the ongoing benevolence of his Director-<u>CEO</u>-Commander. As Leader Replication continues, however, the whole organization is at risk. (Leader Replication will be described in the following pages.)

With Director + Reconciler balance, good things are more likely to happen.

If they will find balance and gain the associated synergy, Director-CEO-Commanders must prayerfully consider the slowing of productivity in favor of Unity, and Reconciler-COO-Executors must prayerfully consider motivating greater productivity in favor of accomplishing goals.

Commander/Executor Balance

The strength of such Director-CEO-Commander/Reconciler-COO-Executor partnerships may be demonstrated by considering the war general Director-Commander who accepts that some number of soldiers must die in battle. If balanced by a Reconciler-Executor in Co-Leadership, the Director-Commander will hear Reconciler-Executor concerns regarding the level of risk upon soldier morale and perhaps agree that the battle plan should be modified. On the other hand, there will likely be occasions when the Reconciler-Executor will need to join in convincing the troops that a greater sacrifice will be needed in this particular battle if they are to win the war.

Such was the relationship between General George Patton and General Matt Eddy during World War II. Both strong alphas, Patton was the Director in the relationship and Eddy was the Reconciler. Patton was heartless and dangerous, but masterful in high-risk strategy. Eddy, called “the voice of reason”, was able to moderate Patton’s flamboyant devil-may-care arrogance. Otherwise excessively risking life, limb and morale, together they were able to lead the Americans to Hitler’s doorstep.

Remembering what was said about Commanders not surviving long term without Executor balance, General Patton was frequently told by President Eisenhower that he was at risk of losing his command. Thank God for

Eisenhower and Eddy, their balancing influence made the most of Patton's strengths - contributing greatly to our winning of World War II.

In The Alpha Male Syndrome, Ludeman and Erlandson describe the inability of any Commander to survive long term without such an appropriate partnership.

Are you a "Patton" style leadership personality? This Director/Commander personality (ENTJ) is only 2% of the population.

Are you an "Eddy" style leadership personality? This Reconciler/Executor personality (ENFJ) is only 3% of the population.

ENTJ and ENFJ are the *Leaders of Leaders* personalities leading our governments and our largest corporations. The people in these positions are responsible for the most important decisions of our day! Can you see how critical it is that they be leading us in Co-Leadership for the bringing and sustaining of balanced decisions at scale?

Chapter Five

Merging Terms:
Director-Rational-Commander &
Reconciler-Idealist-Executor

> You may want to read through these pages a few of times to be sure it sinks in. It will be important as we build upon it moving forward and is necessary in understanding the pursuit of highly productive relational Unity as we scale. Not everyone will follow it easily the first time through, but hopefully the graphics will be helpful in reference.

The MBTI graphic below identifies this complementary difference: High-capacity Directors-Commanders are typically Rationals and high-capacity Reconcilers-Executors are typically Idealists. There is a great potential for balance when these leaders are working together under Co-Leadership and in Mutual Accountability.

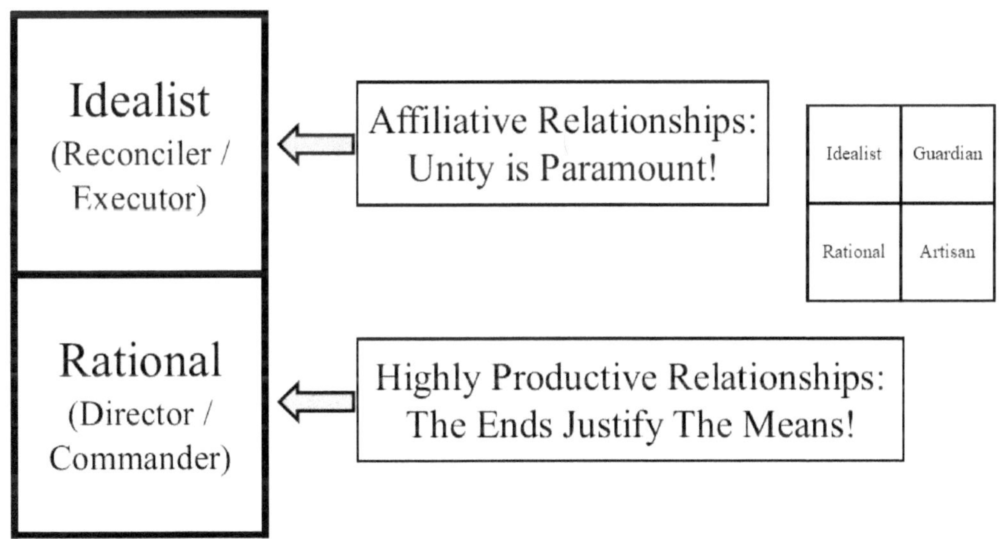

Affiliation and Pragmatism: Preference for Relationship or Productivity?

- Reconcilers-Idealists-Executors prefer affiliation. That is to say that they tend to choose relationships over productivity.

- Directors-Rationals-Commanders prefer pragmatism. That is to say that they tend to choose productivity over relationships.

Further - using all 4 base types:

- Idealists and Guardians both tend toward affiliative relationships: **"Unity is paramount!"**
- Rationals and Artisans both tend toward pragmatic highly productive relationships: "**The ends justify the means**!"

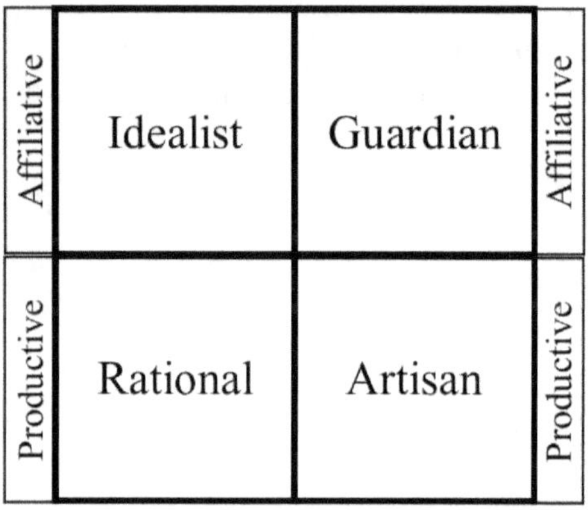

Affiliative	Idealist	Guardian	Affiliative
Productive	Rational	Artisan	Productive

The Abstract and Symbolic or the Concrete and Real? Our Mind's Eye: The following graphic helps us understand that Idealists and Rationals prefer to work with ideas using their envisioning mind. Guardians and Artisans prefer to apply their minds to working with items in the physical realm. All four may be quite creative - in their own realm.

Abstract / Symbolic	Concrete / Real
Idealist	Guardian
Rational	Artisan
Abstract / Symbolic	Concrete / Real

Affiliation or Pragmatism and **Abstract or Concrete**

Merging these graphics into one we get the following:

	Abstract / Symbolic	Concrete / Real	
Affiliative	Idealist	Guardian	Affiliative
Productive	Rational	Artisan	Productive
	Abstract / Symbolic	Concrete / Real	

Director-Rational-Commander & Reconciler-Idealist-Executor

Remembering that the 4 quadrants each have four sub-types, when we put these leaders-of-leaders in their places on the MBTI chart we get the following regarding their preference for:

- giving direction versus offering information
- assertively initiating actions versus preferring to respond in support

	Directive	Informative	Directive	Informative	
Responsive	Idealist		Guardian		Responsive
Assertive	**Reconciler / COO / Executor**				Assertive
Responsive	Rational		Artisan		Responsive
Assertive	**Director / CEO / Commander**				Assertive
	Directive	Informative	Directive	Informative	

Both Directors and Reconcilers are Assertive-Directive. At the base level, neither want to listen to the other, they both want to take Control!

Leader Replication, not Multiplication: Directors
Left unaware of the tendency, Directors-Rationals-Commanders tend to end up with teams of predominantly pragmatic Rationals & Artisans. That is to say that, over time, Rationals-Directors-Commanders tend to weed out the less productive but more relational Idealists & Guardians. Therefore their teams evolve to become *more productive & less relational*.

Leader Replication, not Multiplication: Reconcilers
Left unaware of the tendency, Reconcilers-Idealists-Executors tend to end up with teams of predominantly affiliative Idealists & Guardians. That is to say that, over time, Reconcilers-Idealists-Executors tend to weed out the more productive but less relational Rationals & Artisans. Therefore their teams evolve to become *more relational & less productive*.

It is also important to recognize that, left unaware, we tend to NOT get along well with our MBTI and DiSC opposites (with some exceptions). In MBTI, Artisans & Idealists have a tendency to conflict, and Rationals & Guardians have a tendency to conflict. In DiSC, Dominance & Steadiness have a tendency to conflict and Influence & Conscientiousness have a tendency to conflict. (More information on Pragmatics, Affiliators and Conflict Pairs are available from Inscape Publishing on the web.)

I cannot know all things, so God brings me help in the form of people and information. The Enemy tries to separate us by convincing us to ignore our opposites. But they know some things we do not know, and we need all of the perspectives we can get.

Some will be like Peter, Judas, Nicodemus, the Rich Young Ruler, the religious leaders of the day and the pre-Christian Pharisee Saul. We are not to drive them away, like Jesus we are to point them to the Father while answering their questions and concerns! In close proximity to them, speaking to them with the attitudes of the Beatitudes and in fruit of the Spirit language and actions as described in detail in *Life* - they will find faith or they will run. That is *their* choice!

Peter was opinionated not divisive, and passionate - like most of our high-capacity leaders. We just think they are divisive because they are not submitting to (or maybe not acknowledging of) our *hierarchical position* of Authority and the respect that we believe we are entitled to by virtue *of* that position.

This is a syllogism and FAE that may only be supported by the premise of Authority.

When we attribute ill intentions to another's behavior, we will be able to rationalize conflict avoidance strategies. Therefore, scuttled by this deception, the synergistic potential between complementary personalities will reject Connectivity.

****

Others will simply be well-intentioned Guardians, serving *traditions* in the belief that *these* are *how* they are to support the body of Christ. Not so bad on their own, works may become idols that they serve, doing "good" and therefore *feeling* good about themselves, their identity and their eternity. Something like *faith without works is dead*, they feel they *need* these places of service to feel right about themselves.

Guardians (your traditionalists) make up 46% of the population. Until they *become talmidim*, the various folks serving the congregation through altar, music, accoutrements, lawn & landscape, parking, etc. will, over time, block your path to growing the kingdom of God. That they are not talmidim will be evidenced by cliques that are more social than invitational and transformational. Over the decades, absent appropriate training - you can expect the Enemy to do anything but use it for good – though the *work* is getting done.

A dwindling congregation is symptomatic of a malaise, a short-sightedness, a misunderstanding of appropriate system & structure, and more than anything else – that individuals are not being developed life-on-life to know and understand how to live a life pleasing to God. For if they were, their numbers would be growing as talmidim did what talmidim are to do.

Life, Love and Leading were written to support you with individuals in *life-on-life* time, their *individual* time in worshipful dialogue with Adonai (prayer) and the foundational operating system and structure God has provided us for doing it in Unity as a *fellowship* of believers, a *congregation* of the committed and talmidim who *go* rather than just come.

As visitors recognize that we are not a place doing business, but one where more and more are *living lives pleasing to God* in the Family of God, our talmidim will be more and more successful in drawing in others for training. More than preaching, we will see that the kingdom is growing because of talmidim who are making talmidim in life-on-life services.

Finally, here is your chance for a helpful summary all in one place. Adapted from Working Together by Isachsen & Berens, it is important to understand that we tend to want to have our "meetings" with others *"in" our own quadrant*. That is to say *"on our own turf"* - but that is disastrous. Our interactions with others will always be best served if we will conscientiously meet in the neutrality of the crosshairs of the middle between the four. This is where none of us are "on our own turf" and it is more difficult to posture for Control. In this way, the respect for our complementary differences may add tremendous synergy.

All of the charts in the *Life, Love and Leading* books are available for free download at OneKingdomWorldwide.org

Prefer Thinking & Talking in Symbols, Ideas, Representations & Abstractions | **Prefer Thinking & Talking about the Here & Now, the Real & Concrete (not in Abstracts)**

Affiliation / Consensus / Social Values: Care & Cooperation

IDEALISTS *(16.5% of population)*

Meaning · Significance · Growth: "Becoming" is Most Important

(NFs: ENFJ, INFJ, ENFP, INFP)

The Idealists want to be authentic, benevolent and empathic. They search for identity, meaning and significance. In fact, life is one constant search for identity. They are relationship oriented and they must have meaningful relationships for their life to be worth living. They devote a lot of time to nurturing those relationships. They tend to be romantic, idealistic and want to make the world a better place. They are future oriented. NFs trust their intuition, their imagination and their fantasy. These are as real and significant to them as an actual tree or a chair. Their focus tends to be on developing potential, fostering and facilitating growth through coaching, teaching, counseling and communicating. They will add these dimensions to whatever job they hold. If a job description does not call for these inclinations, they will do these things on their own, often providing a greater value to the organization by virtue of greasing the wheels and defusing tension than the contribution they make doing their prescribed job. Generally, they are enthusiastic, especially about the ideas or causes that interest them. Their natural thinking style is one of integrating and seeing similarities. They look for universal principles and usually hold a global view. NFs are usually gifted in the use of language, oral and written. Metaphors abound in their language and they use this gift to bridge different perspectives and create harmony. Idealists are usually diplomatic, they put their many people and communication talents to work in the service of their ideals and morale.

GUARDIANS *(46.1% of population)*

Membership · Responsibility · Accountability "Serving" is Most Important

(SJs: ESTJ, ISTJ, ESFJ, ISFJ)

The Guardians want to belong, to have membership in whatever group is theirs. They hunger for responsibility and accountability. Frequently, they take on too much responsibility and become overworked. They expect others to work hard and be accountable. They favor generosity, service and duty. They establish and maintain institutions and standard operating procedures. SJs want to preserve the world and protect their charges, so they stand guard, so to speak. They can be found to give warnings when someone or something is going off course or varying too much from the prescribed norm. They look to the past and tradition for security and standards. Frequently, they foster enculturation with ceremonies, rules and rituals. Guardians trust contracts and authority and distrust chance. The want security and stability. SJs think in terms of convention, association and discrete elements, and thus emphasize memory and drill as paths to mastery. Generally they are serious and concerned, with a fatalistic stance. Guardians are skilled at ensuring that things and people are in the right place, in the right amounts, the right quality and at the right time. Frequently, they gravitate towards business and commerce, especially in the areas where safekeeping and logistics are required.

Affiliation / Consensus / Social Values: Care & Cooperation

The neutral turf where we respectfully exchange ideas and find synergy in agreement.

Pragmatism / Autonomy / Use of Power for Expediency

RATIONALS *(10.4% of population)*

Competence · Intellect · Vision: "Knowing" is Most Important

(NTs: ENTJ, INTJ, ENTP, INTP)

The Rationals seek knowledge, competence, and achievement. They strive to understand what makes the world run and people tick. Rationals are fascinated by and drawn to theories. Everything is conditional and relative to the context in which it is found or expressed. Like the Idealists, they are future oriented. They trust logic and reason. Everything must be logical and proceed from carefully defined premises. Rationals want to have a rationale for everything and are natural skeptics. They think in terms of differences, delineating categories, definitions, structures and functions. If their job is too routine, they formulate hypotheses and theories to make it interesting. They hunger for precision, especially in thought and language. Long-range planning, inventing, designing and defining are their areas of strength and they bring these gifts to any job even if they are not called for. Their mood is generally calm and they prefer a peaceful environment. They foster individualism rather than conformity. Frequently they gravitate toward technology and the sciences and are well suited for engineering and devising strategy.

ARTISANS *(27% of population)*

Action · Grace · Spontaneity: "Doing" is Most Important

(SPs: ESTP, ISTP, ESFP, ISFP)

Artisans want the freedom to choose their next act. They must experience and act on impulses. They want to be graceful, bold and impressive and to have an impact on their "audience". They are generally excited and optimistic, expecting lady luck to be on their side. SPs may become so absorbed in the action of the moment that they lose sight of distant goals. The flip side: they see opportunities that others miss (which they seize if at all possible). Artisans are oriented toward the present and they seek adventure and experiences. They hunger for spontaneity. SPs trust their impulses, luck and their ability to solve any problem they run into. Thus, they frequently rush in when others hold back with fear and hesitation. Artisans are natural negotiators and enjoy getting others to concede even some small part. They think in terms of variation, thus the name Artisan. The capacity for producing variations on a theme shows up in all that they do, not just in the limited sense of "arts and crafts". No matter what their job, they will find some way to vary it. They have a keen ability to notice and describe detail. They like the freedom to move, festivities and games. Gifted tacticians, figuring out the best move to make at the instant, Artisans do the expedient thing, not the acceptable, friendly or logical thing. Frequently they are drawn to the manual, visual and performing arts as well as entrepreneurial aspects of business.

Pragmatism / Autonomy / Use of Power for Expediency

Prefer Thinking & Talking in Symbols, Ideas, Representations & Abstractions | **Prefer Thinking & Talking about the Here & Now, the Real & Concrete (not in Abstracts)**

Prefer to be Directive and give Directives (NJ & ST): INFJ, ENFJ, INTJ, ENTJ, ISTJ, ESTJ, ISTP, ESTP
Prefer to be Informative and give Information (NP & SF): INFP, ENFP, INTP, ENTP, ISFJ, ESFJ, ISFP, ESFP

Our interactions with others will always be best served if we will conscientiously meet in the neutrality of the crosshairs of the middle between the four. This is where none of us are "on our own turf" and it is more difficult to posture for Control.

We have decisions to make every day of our lives. Until we understand the value of his Unity OS and our complementary differences, we will continue to make our decisions along the scale opposites of patience & impatience and love of self & love of others. Determined to get what *we* want, we will also be willing to use the *manipulate to control* strategies needed to *get* what we want!

As we learn to synergize with others – and get more than we could have imagined on our own - these destructive flip-side tendencies slowly fade into the background. No longer right-handed or left-handed, we become ambidextrous and far more capable in coordinating our movement collaboratively with others. The end result is that we *become* far more productive than when we were attempting to lead on our own.

Chapter Six

Understanding Director/Reconciler Conflict

At a base level, the typical conflict between high-capacity Directors (typically Rationals) and high capacity Reconcilers (typically Idealists) centers around the speed of change or the type of change, and its impact upon the lives of the people involved. Those who want to move quickly do not want to sit around and talk about it. Those who want to talk about sustainable relationships see the risk in expediency.

While Directors-Rationals-Commanders tend to select for a balance of productivity first and relational compatibility second, Reconcilers-Idealists-Executors tend to select for relational compatibility first and productivity second. In decision making, we not only have facts to consider and strategies toward accomplishment of vision, but we also have pace of implementation issues that will affect relational sustainability. These require a balanced D+R outlook that will therefore balance our decision-making.

Further, as was identified in the previous chapter, Directors-Rationals-Commanders and Reconcilers-Idealists-Executors are both Assertive-Directive. That is, they are both used to *being* followed, not following. Each will do their level best to gain or regain Control, and as was detailed in *Life*, Reconcilers-Idealists-Executors are typically the first to back down.

Very importantly, Meyers-Briggs identifies the *Order of Preferences* the 16 types *tend to use* when considering any given decision. While it will be very helpful for you to understand the four areas listed below, what is most important in *this* discussion is to recognize that all four are needed for a balanced decision, and that we all have our own order and processes for going through them.

What follows are those for the ENFJ Reconciler-Idealist-Executor and the ENTJ Director-Rational-Commander:

Order Of Prefences:
ENFJ vs ENTJ

ENFJ	ENTJ
1. Feeling	1. Thinking
2. Intuition	2. Intuition
3. Sensing	3. Sensing
4. Thinking	4. Feeling

What we see here is that the *last* thing an ENTJ (Director-Rational-Commander) does is consider Feelings when compared to what they *Think* about it, and the *last* thing an ENFJ (Reconciler-Idealist-Executor) does is consider what they Think in comparison to their *Feelings* about it. *If either do it at all!*

So many of us "go with our gut" in decision-making, meaning that we don't fully consider all four areas. In fact, the Order Of Preferences calls our 1st Priority our Dominant Priority and our 4th (last) priority in decision-making our Inferior Priority. Many of us have already made our decisions by the time we finish considering our 2nd Preference, and are therefore not easily persuaded afterward to *adjust* that decision.

We need others to help us strengthen our 3rd and 4th Preferences in decision-making. Clearly, Directors need Executors and vice versa. This has tremendous implications!

Though we prefer operating more as one of the three versus the other two, situationally we must endeavor to balance, mature and make ready for use each portion of our Director/Reconciler/Active Implementer selves. If we will allow the sanctification of the Holy Spirit to occur through our experiences and the Mutual Accountability offered by those around us, *Adonai* will produce in us maturity between our Director/Reconciler/Active Implementer selves. He will help us mature such that we do not go with our gut, but seek out our opposites to hear what they have to say about it. These include those whose Order Of Preferences are opposite ours.

Directors can strengthen their Reconciler/Active Implementer muscles. Reconcilers can strengthen their Director/Active Implementer muscles. Active Implementers can strengthen their Director/Reconciler muscles. This is maturity. This is what happens through sanctification. This is what brings us balance and develops each "muscle" in our Order Of Preferences. This therefore brings balance in our Director/Reconciler/Active Implementer selves. Our ability to recognize what the situation before us calls for requires our mature ability to apply any of the three.

This is extremely important in the marriage relationship. More often than not, the Order Of Preferences for each spouse are quite opposite. During the dating phase, this ability to see things from differing perspectives in a Gentle and helpful way were part of what drew them together. Later, after several years of marriage, these significantly contribute to what is commonly called The Seven Year Itch: that which was formerly drawing has now begun to repel. The one who Thinks first has a hard time with the one who is Feeling first. "How can you say that? That doesn't make any sense!", "Well how can *you* say *that*? It sounds cold and cruel!"

If each will remember the Order Of Preferences and ask the other the clarifying question, "Help me understand why you are saying...." understanding will more easily be achieved and the quality of the outcome dramatically improved. Otherwise, we will find ourselves at a *standstill*, the place where no decision can be made *together* - and where *manipulate to Control strategies* are frequently contemplated by each side.

This is where we are politically, and where we have been going <u>more and more</u> during the last two decades.

When we truly take the time to work through our Preferences together, the other side may again be valued for their differences – and our decisions and relationships strengthened: 2 Corinthians 3:18 *<u>more and more</u>, little by little, bit by bit, glory by glory.*

It is all part of the cosmic battle between God and Evil for the Control of the world. It is all part of the cosmic battle between God and Evil for individual souls. Who will change the discourse? Will you be a part of the solution for the lives of our children? For the future leaders of the world? Pray for the children!

****

When we Unite diverse *types* into given *roles*, good things are more likely to happen. Those under Individuated Leadership will always suffer until the other half of the D+R leadership team is found and their value respected. Team strength will always be improved by the inclusion of all of the temperaments: Rationals, Idealists, Guardians and Artisans.

Science is learning and proving God's way. Made as imagers, we are Directors, Reconcilers and Active Implementers. Leaders are Directors and Reconcilers. Those in Supportive Service are typically Active Implementers, some of whom are young Directors and Reconcilers trying to find their way into small scale leadership with an eye toward larger scale leadership.

To be clear, we are all Directors, Reconcilers and Active Implementers - though we tend to prefer to major in one of these roles rather than the other two. Rationals, Idealists, Guardians and Artisans are all capable of leadership roles, though high-capacity (alpha) leaders tend to be Rationals and Idealists (25% of the population). That is to say that Guardians and Artisans are most often leaders of a few or leaders of many while Rationals and Idealists may more often be leaders of leaders. The greater point in all cases is the level of our maturity as Christ followers. Powerful Directors with little Reconciler maturity will be dangerous leaders. Passionate Reconcilers with little Director maturity will not be very productive.

Again, though we prefer operating more as one of the three versus the other two, situationally we must endeavor to balance, mature and make ready for use each portion of our Director/Reconciler/Active Implementer selves. If we will allow the sanctification of the Holy Spirit to occur through our experiences and the Mutual Accountability offered by those around us, *Adonai* will produce in us maturity within our Director/Reconciler/Active Implementer selves.

Otherwise, our house divided against itself will continue to wobble as we use our sophisticated tools of manipulation to Divide, Conquer, Slander and Control.

Mark 3:24-25

24 If a kingdom is divided against itself, that kingdom cannot stand. 25 And if a house is divided against itself, that house will not be able to stand.

2 Corinthians 3:17-18

17 Now the Lord is the Spirit, and where the Spirit of the Lord is, there is freedom. 18 And we all, with unveiled face, beholding the glory of the Lord, are being transformed into the same image from one degree of glory to another. For this comes from the Lord who is the Spirit.

Romans 8:26-29

*26 Likewise the Spirit helps us in our weakness. For we do not know what to
pray for as we ought, but the Spirit himself intercedes for us with groanings
too deep for words. 27 And he who searches hearts knows what is the mind
of the Spirit, because the Spirit intercedes for the saints according to the will
of God. 28 And we know that for those who love God all things work
together for good, for those who are called according to his purpose. 29 For
those whom he foreknew he also predestined to be conformed to the image of
his Son, in order that he might be the firstborn among many brothers.*

John 6:45

It is written in the Prophets, 'And they will all be taught by God.' Everyone who has heard and learned from the Father comes to me.

John 14:10

Do you not believe that I am in the Father and the Father is in me? The words that I say to you I do not speak on my own authority, but the Father who dwells in me does his works.

1 Corinthians 2: 10, 12, 13, 14, 16

*10 these things God has revealed to us through the Spirit. For the Spirit
searches everything, even the depths of God. 12 Now we have received not
the spirit of the world, but the Spirit who is from God, that we might
understand the things freely given us by God. 13 And we impart this in
words not taught by human wisdom but taught by the Spirit, interpreting
spiritual truths to those who are spiritual. 14 The natural person does not
accept the things of the Spirit of God, for they are folly to him, and he is not
able to understand them because they are spiritually discerned. 16 "For
who has understood the mind of the Lord so as to instruct him?"
But we have the mind of Christ.*

Galatians 5:16-26

*16 But I say, walk by the Spirit, and you will not gratify the desires of the
flesh. 17 For the desires of the flesh are against the Spirit, and the desires of
the Spirit are against the flesh, for these are opposed to each other, to keep
you from doing the things you want to do. 18 But if you are led by the
Spirit, you are not under the law. 19 Now the works of the flesh are evident:
sexual immorality, impurity, sensuality, 20 idolatry, sorcery, enmity, strife,*

jealousy, fits of anger, rivalries,
dissensions, divisions, 21 envy, drunkenness, orgies, and things like these. I warn you, as I warned you before, that those who (continue to) do such things will not inherit the kingdom of God. 22 But the fruit of the Spirit is love, joy, peace, patience, kindness, goodness, faithfulness, 23 gentleness, self-control; against such things there is no law. 24 And those who belong to Christ Jesus have crucified the flesh with its passions and desires. 25 If we live by the Spirit, let us also keep in step with the Spirit. 26 Let us not become conceited, provoking one another, envying one another.

Shared Leadership using the Totality of Available Input: Churches
Director Senior Pastors speed along productively for the greater good. Reconciler Senior Pastors slow the pace of productivity in favor of sustainable relationships. This is also true for boards/councils/elders that are imbalanced Director *groups* or Reconciler *groups*. In any case, whenever board/council/elder groups are in place hierarchically above pastors – Authoritarian conflict and disunity are inevitable. These churches are utilizing a Parallels OS (See Chapter Seven of *Life*) and should endeavor to transition back to the "Staff Are Elders" model that we had as church plants before we scaled. This will be described at length as we proceed.

Whenever board/council/elder groups are in place hierarchically – Authoritarian conflict and disunity are inevitable.

To balance productivity and relationships in determination of the *appropriate pace or speed*, there must be a process whereby any and all may be assured of being heard and respected. ALL must be given a full and fair opportunity for input. Most leaders would say they are fair in that regard, but our FAEs, syllogisms and Director/Reconciler selves tend toward something else because we are often not aware of the tendency.

The wise utilize diverse groups of giftedness in regular Advisory Forums to listen to whatever may be said by anyone on any subject. If I do not do that, my personal tendencies may easily cause me to miss the point of what is being said by a complementary opposite. Herein lies one of the many big risks with Individuated Leadership, we end up as gatekeepers filtering out God's alpha Supporters, Disruptors and Correctors – sent for our Help and Encouragement. As we "*continue to" attempt to Control* people and events -

leaning on our own understanding - we do not have eyes that see or ears that hear.

Matthew 13:14-15

14 Indeed, in their case the prophecy of Isaiah is fulfilled that says: “‘“You will indeed hear but never understand, and you will indeed see but never perceive.” 15 For this people's heart has grown dull, and with their ears they can barely hear, and their eyes they have closed, lest they should see with their eyes and hear with their ears and understand with their heart and turn, and I would heal them.’

Unfortunately, the percentage of churches utilizing Spiritual Gifts along with MBTI, DiSC, StrengthsFinder and Alpha assessments is small. Others use outdated MBTI information to little advantage. It is simply irresponsible to leave refined and reliable personality science out of our church organization and operating system. Science has helped us prove that God quickly created the universe in seven days through the sort of “Big Bang” that science and Genesis describe. Personality science and consultative experts are also helping us with practical insights into our triune personalities - that we might operate together in One-ness – Adonai-ically.

In their eyes, Jeremiah was a troublemaker. David was only there to deliver lunch when he offered to slay Goliath. Jesse had David stay behind to tend the sheep while his brothers were brought to Samuel for consideration as the next king.

Herein lies one of the many big risks with Individuated Leadership: we end up as gatekeepers filtering out God’s alpha Supporters, Disruptors and Correctors – sent for our Help and Encouragement. As we “continue to” attempt to Control people and events - leaning on our own understanding - we do not have eyes that see or ears that hear.

Chapter Seven

Balancing Leader Multiplication

Let's take a look at how balanced Director and Reconciler Co-Leadership succeeds during Leader *Multiplication.*

In Co-Leadership, staff invitations occur by consensus. If the Director(s) and Reconciler(s) disagree, no invitation occurs. In this way, the only people invited are identified by both the Director(s) and the Reconciler(s) as mature and balanced in their productive and relational character. They are additionally intentional about growing a full complement of Director, Reconciler, Guardian, Artisan, Rational and Idealist giftedness such that ALL of the information from the perspectives of the 4 quadrants will be heard during decision-making. Otherwise, we tend to not want to include our D/R, MBTI and DiSC opposites.

If leader *replication* occurs instead of leader *multiplication*, we begin to have fewer and fewer of our opposites available to disagree with us. While that may seem to improve Unity, it is at the expense of some of the information we need in discernment and therefore decision-making. As decisions are made with less than the full complement of data, mistakes are more often made.

Later we will discuss the rise and fall of a fast growing Unity Operated church plant that fell victim to this during Leader Multiplication. As Leader Multiplication became Leader Replication, and upon achieving a very large scale, it eventually crashed in a highly public way.

Productive *and* Relational

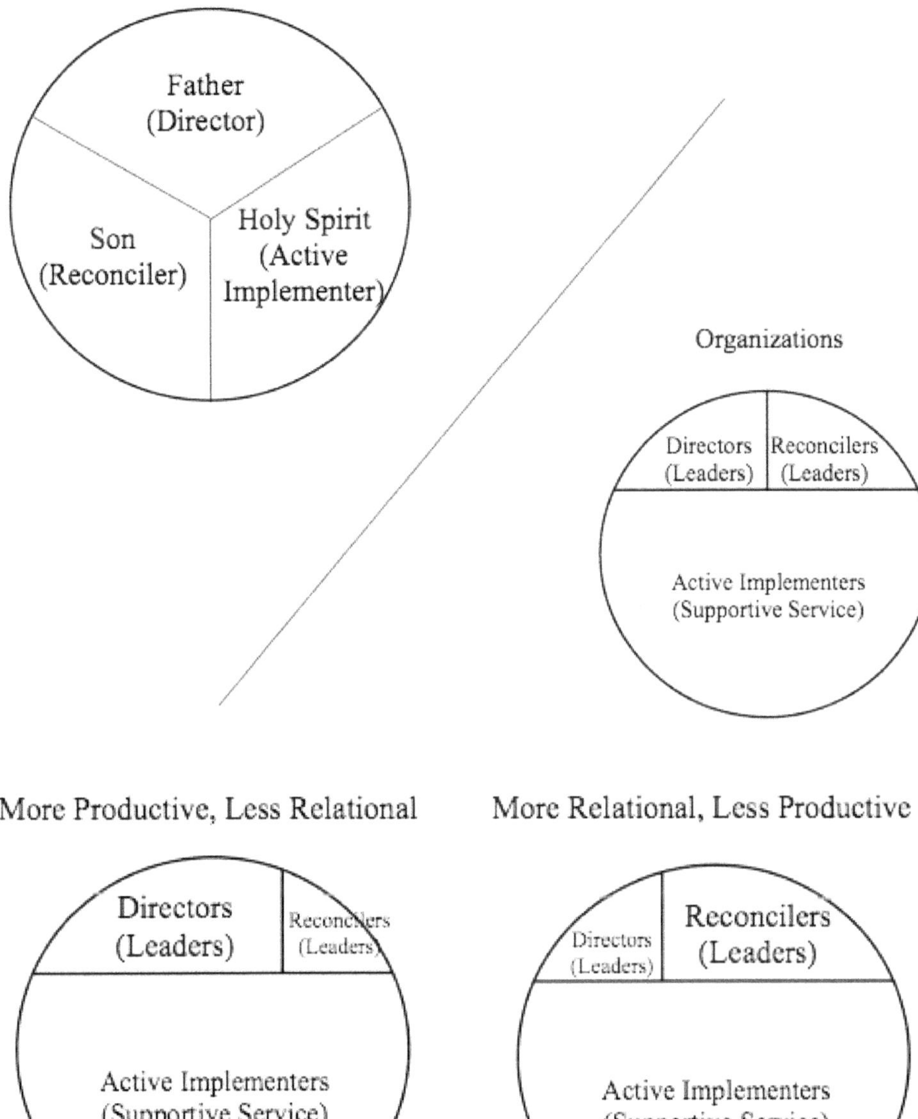

In the hierarchical World Operating System, we assume Control with all of the best of intentions and then tend to either speed along productively in relational conflict or move along more slowly in relational Unity. Collateral relational damage occurs when we race along too quickly with productivity that we call good - seemingly expecting God to accept it as necessary – but that is not his way.

Matthew 7:22-23

22 On that day many will say to me, 'Lord, Lord, did we not prophesy in your name, and cast out demons in your name, and do many mighty works in your name?' 23 And then will I declare to them, 'I never knew you; depart from me, you workers of lawlessness.'

There's nothing wrong with having drive, but there is everything wrong with being Driven. The drive that helps us to push on and Persevere when our Adversary is causing us trouble is one thing. But it is Enemy induced for disunity when productivity *drives us* to rationalize that it is necessary to push past our Correctors and Disruptors. Some of us are extremely adept at feigning dialogue while actually *pressuring for buy-in* as we *man*age, *man*ipulate and *man*euver for rubber stamps.

As the World Operating System tells us that there can only be one boss, it is a short and easy step to advise our high-capacity alpha brothers and sisters to accept that I have been given the Authority, that I am the one responsible to make it all happen and that they are the ones who are going to need to respect that and take a step back.

There is much to be gained in the conversational process of respectful Dialogue over disagreement. This is where *iron sharpens iron*, Relational Mutual Accountability occurs, Co-Discipleship is offered, eyes are opened, ears hear and – unfortunately – *time* is lost. But time itself belongs to the Father, even Jesus doesn't know the timing of his return! Following in his ways, we are to prioritize relational Unity over expedient productivity and trust him *collectively* for Direction, Pace *and* Timing.

I recall the church whose elders all agreed that God was leading a significant revision and new alignment in their schedule of services. In agreement, they began working through the various options for implementation and also came into agreement that God was identifying a particular option. All in agreement about the what and the how, all that remained was the when. It took an additional five years before all came into agreement that it was finally the Father's timing for when! As they looked back at how the events of the previous five years had unfolded, they were thankful that they had not moved before receiving his confirmation on timing. Now, years after its implementation, it has gone better than they could have ever imagined!

****

In the above example regarding the timing of implementation of what had been agreed upon, you can bet that an Individuated Director (or Director team) would have moved ahead with it on his (their) own – at his (their) peril! The Authoritarian World Operating System will never have Unity of action *and Timing*, but we Christ followers can have it now. Some of us already do.

As we have seen, organizations in Leader Replication look more and more like themselves and result in roller coasters of conflict over time. We hire Director Senior Pastors or Reconciler Senior Pastors and then eventually find fault with them relationally or with insufficient productivity. It is not God's design that we would use unbalanced Individuated Leadership and Authority to lead the coming of his Kingdom. *Christ* is the Head, we are all just Body Parts led by the Holy Spirit for works created long ago.

Ecclesiastes 4:9-12

9 Two are better than one, because they have a good reward for their toil. 10 For if they fall, one will lift up his fellow. But woe to him who is alone when he falls and has not another to lift him up! 11 Again, if two lie together, they keep warm, but how can one keep warm alone? 12 And though a man might prevail against one who is alone, two will withstand him—a threefold cord is not quickly broken.

I have been blessed to observe churches under highly productive and relational Director+Reconciler Co-Leadership in differing organizational styles. In each case the Directors and Reconcilers had matured in such Christ-likeness that it was difficult to tell which was which. All were Visionary. All were Strategic. All seemed capable of Command, but did not need to use it. All were effectively Executing due to their adherence to Unity At All Costs and inclusion of all of the information from all of the people. The Spirit was truly leading with Christ the Head - not them. They made it look easy. Made as imagers and committed to One-ness, Mutual

Accountability had brought balance to their Director/Reconciler/Active Implementer selves - and Joy to the Body.

Given our productivity bias and value for expediency, most of us continue to exclude important information sources due to our Foundational Operating Errors – and Unity is tossed to and fro by Authoritarian error.

The Enemy deceived Israel long ago such that the elders told Samuel to tell God they wanted a king. The World Operating System seemed simpler, more efficient and required less time in meetings. Decisions could be made more quickly – in the interest of time. But time has proven to be our enemy as the hierarchical World OS became deeply engrained in our cultures. Nevertheless, we have the benefit of hindsight they couldn't have. God used the past for us in preparation for *our* future and *his* Kingdom that came once – and is now *in the process of coming* again on earth as it is in heaven.

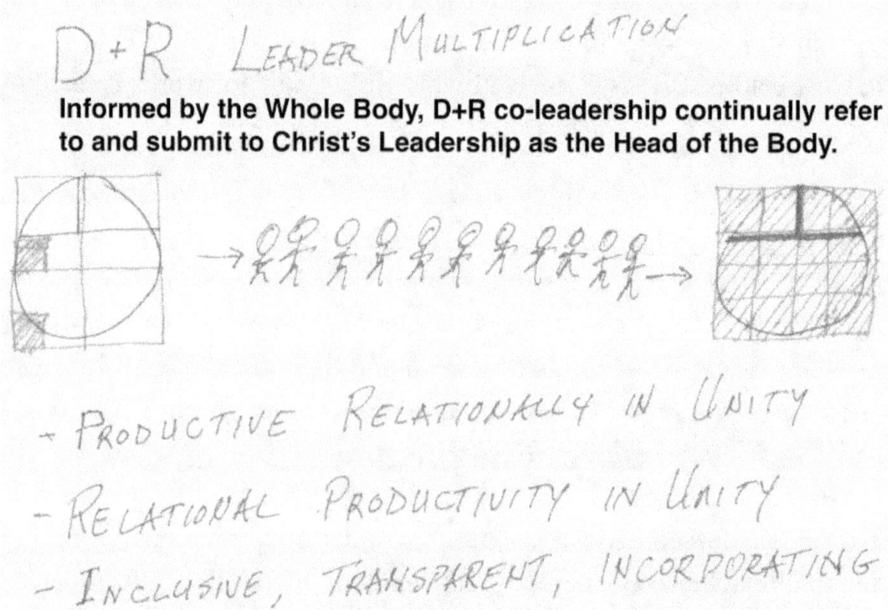

Chapter Eight

It's Biblical: Co-Leadership

His-story (the Bible) shows us that the Enemy's deceptive World Operating System and Structure continues to cause the same mistakes the same way every time – though we expect something to change (The definition of insanity!).

Myriad Old Testament passages identify the failures of Individuated Authority (for example the prophets in Judges and kings in Kings) and the successes of Directors who consulted in partnership with their Reconcilers (like Pharaoh/Joseph, Moses/Aaron, Nebuchadnezzar/Nehemiah and some of the King/Prophet tandems).

Evidence Abounds: Directors, Reconcilers, Active Implementers

The following is a very basic chronology of God teaching us the Co-Leadership portion of his Unity Operating System. Each time he has set it up it has been successful. But then the Enemy's hierarchical World OS is always around us for comparison – seducing us. It tempts Lead Leaders to assume power, *take* Authority and *take* charge because it just plain looks faster, better and more efficient – and so we slide back into it. But eventually, individuated leaders always fail in their individuated Authority.

When God sent Director Moses and Reconciler Aaron to Pharaoh to free his people, he was also showing us the way he wants us to lead together. Later, Joshua could not take over the Director role of Moses without the anointing of the Reconciler Eleazar. As we proceed through the Book of Judges we see that Reconciler priests were unable to sustain Individuated Leadership. As we proceed through Samuel and they demand of God a king, individuated Saul fails. As Reconciler Prophets went to king after king to warn them of the mistakes they were making – most kings felt no need to heed because they were "King". The rare king who succeeded typically had the wisdom to heed God's advice through a Reconciler prophet. It should also be noted that Director prophets misdirected kings under the guise of sharing God's word and God's will. Individuated Leadership is unsustainable. The Old Testament is full of this truth, as is all of history.

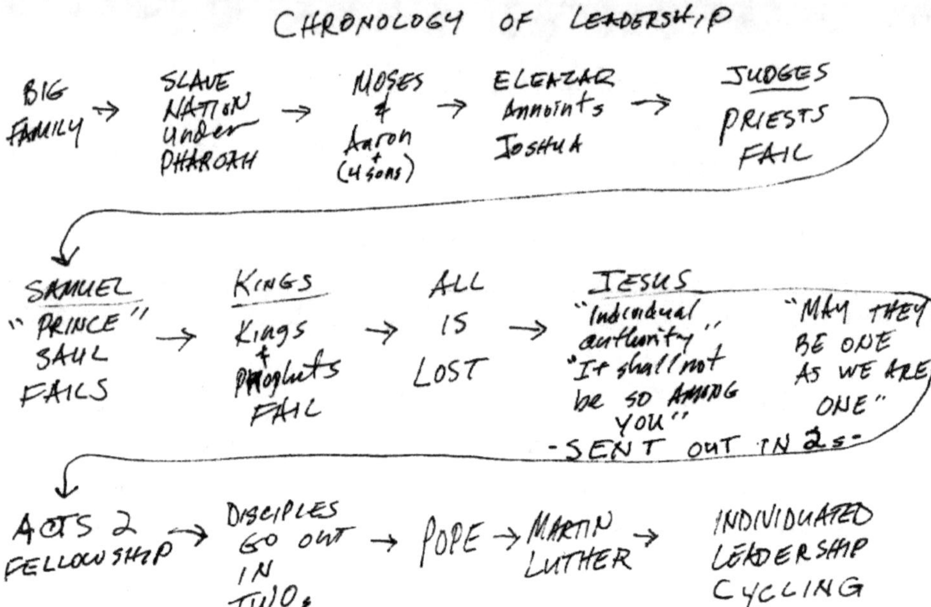

*MAN*agement is not God's way. Under *MAN*agement, (the hierarchical World OS) even the very best of us end up *MAN*ipulating others as we *MAN*euver to gain or sustain Control. We just can't do it any other way when we lead alone. For centuries God has let us try and fail, but what have we learned?

Made in God's image, Adam and Eve were Directors, Reconcilers and Active Implementers. As we know, husbands tend to take the lead and direct some things and wives tend to take the lead to direct others. Husbands and wives discuss and reconcile the leadership of the other with their own ideas of what should be actively implemented. It can be a beautiful thing: Co-Leadership. Unity of Action. One-ness. And as we also know, it fails without Unity with God.

Telling the story in these terms, Eve assimilated the information from the Serpent along with the information (command) provided by God and decided that testing what the Serpent said would be a good idea. She directed Adam to taste the Fruit of the Tree of Knowledge, and - having heard the testimony of God, the Serpent and Eve – Adam reconciled his position to hers, deciding that it would be good to actively implement the test. They both ate, failing to choose Unity with God, and Self-Selected themselves out into the world where they passed the Enemy's World Operating System down to their children and children's children.

Separated from Unity with God, there was no one else to teach them but the Enemy and themselves – for generation after generation after generation.

God provided Adam and Eve Directional Leadership while they were in the Garden. He Advised (commanded) them not to eat the fruit of the Tree of Knowledge lest they surely die. The Serpent's Directional Leadership recommended a life in which the fruit of the Tree of Knowledge would make them like God. Much of humanity utilizes knowledge similarly to this day, in great risk and with the same looming peril.

Exodus 34:7
, keeping steadfast love for thousands, forgiving iniquity and transgression and sin, but who will by no means clear the guilty, visiting the iniquity of the fathers on the children and the children's children, to the third and the fourth generation."

They left Eden and became families using the World OS of Satan's Deception. They maintained their individuated ways with their families – their children observing these ways as they grew up – producing a sense of normality that decisions may be made apart from the input of others. Since the beginning of time, we have been being trained in the use of decision-making according to the World OS.

Without traveling too far, these young adults went out on their own, becoming a family of many families, with each Actively Implementing Authority over people and their portion of the abundant land they came to control beyond Eden. Unresolved disagreements could easily remain unresolved as individuals left the proximity of others for a place of their own choosing – and the freedom to direct and actively implement as they pleased.

They went from being Directors over their family farms to becoming Directors for those under their employ. As was described in detail in *Life*, some were benevolent and fair with their employees, and some used that power to subtly or not so subtly *MAN*ipulate their employees. Subtle and not so subtle *MAN*agement threats to their employment are all the Leverage most leaders need to maintain Control over them. (A strategy we still use today.) Afterall, who wants to risk the income their family needs for food and shelter?

Come to me. My yoke is easy, my burden light.
Imagine with me the evolution of a currency and trading system as population density increased and some were found to be gifted for work on the farm, on the ranch, in fishing or in accumulating items for sale in a shop. It became quite common to put other people's children to work on/in their own farms, ranches, boats and shops in exchange for currency, food and/or shelter. As land became scarce locally, people would travel further to find new land. On the original family tracts, they began to build insulas (clusters of buildings where extended families live together) for their married children rather than lose them and their grandchildren to distance, and so as to allow for the passing on of the "family farm". As our population grew, the inheritance system, the trading of work for food and shelter, and the development of currency systems allowed some to amass great power and wealth.

It went on this way for a thousand years, deeply engraining the Enemy's hierarchical World OS before God intervened with Noah and eventually Moses. Having proven that they could not understand his ways and had no hope of ever doing so, he gave them the 10 Commandments and began to show us our way back home.

Now take what we have learned in the preceding pages about our personalities, giftedness and Individuated Authority tendencies - along with their ignorance of it – and you will quickly see how old the culture of the hierarchical World OS is and how right it seemed to them. And seems to *us*. But the burden is so very heavy.

Matthew 11:28-30
28 Come to me, all who labor and are heavy laden, and I will give you rest. 29 Take my yoke upon you, and learn from me, for I am gentle and lowly in heart, and you will find rest for your souls. 30 For my yoke is easy, and my burden is light."

Philippians 4:5b-7
5b... The Lord is at hand; 6 do not be anxious about anything, but in everything by prayer and supplication with thanksgiving let your requests be

made known to God. 7 <u>And the peace of God, which surpasses all understanding, will guard your hearts and your minds in Christ Jesus</u>.

How heavy is the yoke of your Authoritarian leadership experience? If you are heavy laden, it is likely because you have placed the excess burden of the World OS upon yourself (or let others do so to you) and are going it more or less alone. As you may know, the yoke he describes is the type with two holes in it – one for the older mature ox and one for the younger ox in training. Individuated Leaders leave his yoke behind (the one where God does the work while training us) and use a one hole version instead - going their own way, in their own strength, leaning on their own understanding. (For a while anyway.)

Proverbs 3:5-8

5 Trust in the Lord <u>with all your heart</u>, and <u>do not lean on your own understanding</u> (mind). 6 In all your ways acknowledge him, and <u>he</u> will make straight your paths. 7 <u>Be not wise in your own eyes</u> (mind); fear the Lord, and turn away from evil. 8 <u>It will be healing to your flesh and refreshment to your bones</u>.

Scripture shows us what God intended, but though we know these verses we have not been able to live them because we adulterate his system. When our groups compel us to individuate, an Authoritarian cycle begins. That leads to the corruption God described to Samuel back when the elders demanded a king. Then, as over the decades the wheels fall off, it ends with attitudes returning to a desire for Unity. Unfortunately, from there we once again begin to slide back into the belief that we will need to take Control, and utilize Hierarchy & Authority in order to expedite productivity:

Unity collaborating-synergizing-cohesive-responsive-effective-growing-scaling-confusing-conflicting-dividing-usurping Authority control-pride-loss-dysfunction-defensive-faultfinding-ignoring-dismissive-opaque-callous-assuming-rationalizing-marginalizing-ineffective-imploding-inquiring-including-accomodating-envisioning - temporary return to Unity

Mark 9:33-35

33 And they came to Capernaum. And when he was in the house he asked them, "What were you discussing on the way?" 34 But they kept silent, for on the way they had argued with one another about <u>who was the greatest</u>. 35 And he sat down and called the twelve. And he said to them, "If anyone would be first, he must be last of all and servant of all."

Who was greatest among them could only have been important in the determination of who had the most power, and therefore the ability to use it. If I am greater than you then you need to follow my lead – and I will be in Control.

Mark 10:42-45

42 And Jesus called them to him and said to them, "You know that those who are considered rulers of the Gentiles <u>lord it over them</u>, and their <u>great</u> ones <u>exercise authority</u> over them. 43 But <u>it shall not be so among you</u>. But whoever would be great among you must be your servant, 44 and whoever would be first among you must be slave of all. 45 For even the Son of Man came not to be served but to serve, and to give his life as a ransom for many."

We do not need any power or Authority to accomplish the above and following commandments:

Mark 12:28-34a

28 And one of the scribes came up and heard them disputing with one another, and seeing that he answered them well, asked him, "Which commandment is the most important of all?" 29 Jesus answered, "The most important is, 'Hear, O Israel: The Lord our God, the Lord is one. 30 And you shall love the Lord your God with all your heart and with all your soul and with all your mind and with all your strength.' 31 The second is this: 'You shall love your neighbor as yourself.' There is no other commandment greater than these." 32 And the scribe said to him, "You are right, Teacher. You have truly said that he is one, and there is no other besides him. 33 And to love him with all the heart and with all the understanding and with all the strength, and to love one's neighbor as oneself, is much more than all whole burnt offerings and sacrifices." 34 And when Jesus saw that he answered wisely, he said to him "You are not far from the kingdom of God."

Under our power and Authority these Love Commands suffer, and Jesus' prayer to the Father for us will not be realized:

John 17:20-23

20 "I do not ask for these only, <u>but also for those who will believe in me through their word, 21 that they may all be one</u>, just as you, Father, are in me, and I in you, that they also may be in us, so that the world may believe that you have sent me. 22 The glory that you have given me I have given to them, <u>that they may be one even as we are one</u>, 23 I in them and you in me, that they may <u>become perfectly one</u>, so that the world may know that you sent me and loved them even as you loved me.

Chapter Nine

Collective Leadership

Ephesians 4:11-16

11 And he gave the apostles, the prophets, the evangelists, the shepherds and teachers, 12 to equip the saints for the work of ministry, for building up the body of Christ, 13 until we all attain to the unity of the faith and of the knowledge of the Son of God, to mature manhood, to the measure of the stature of the fullness of Christ, 14 so that we may no longer be children, tossed to and fro by the waves and carried about by every wind of doctrine, by human cunning, by craftiness in deceitful schemes.
15 Rather, speaking the truth in love, we are to grow up in every way into him who is the head, into Christ, 16 from whom the whole body, joined and held together by every joint with which it is equipped, when each part is working properly, makes the body grow so that it builds itself up in love.

Note that we are to equip the saints for the work of ministry, support our employees in their work-service and no longer be children, tossed to and fro by the waves - carried about by every wind of doctrine, by human cunning, by craftiness in deceitful schemes. *MANipulation*! We are instead to teach them to observe all that *he* has commanded, because all Authority in heaven and on earth has been given to *him* – not *us*.

Matthew 28:18-20

18 And Jesus came and said to them, "All authority in heaven and on earth has been given to me. 19 Go therefore and make disciples of all nations, baptizing them in the name of the Father and of the Son and of the Holy Spirit, 20 teaching them to observe all that I have commanded you. And behold, I am with you always, to the end of the age."

Colossians 2:8

See to it that no one takes you captive by philosophy and empty deceit, according to human tradition (use of Authority and hierarchy in the Military Chain of Command), according to the elemental spirits of the world (the World OS), and not according to Christ.

God told Adam and Eve that they would surely die if they ate from the Tree of Knowledge. He commanded them not to eat from it for their own benefit. We, too, command others for their own benefit. We command them to do and not do things because (we think) we have *Authority* and vision and responsibility and the bigger picture to consider. But there is a great difference between us doing that and God doing that, we only *think* we know. *We prophecy in part. We cannot see clearly on our own*:

1 Corinthians 13:9-12 NIV
9 For we know in part and we prophesy in part, 10 but when completeness comes, what is in part disappears. 11 When I was a child, I talked like a child, I thought like a child, I reasoned like a child. When I became a man, I put the ways of childhood behind me. 12 For now we see only a reflection as in a mirror; then we shall see face to face. Now I know in part; then I shall know fully, even as I am fully known.

When we as leaders direct, we should be simply directing others' attention to a given *subject for discussion*. Our thoughts on the subject must be recognized by all others as our *suggestions* so as to facilitate *iron sharpening iron* opportunities. In this way the involvement of each will contribute to the framing of the *whole* story. When finally the process is complete, each person will have had the opportunity to Reconcile their individual positions to the clearer understanding of the collective wisdom. By so doing, the final decision will have been developed through the help of *God in us*, and by his leading *for us*.

For him is under our power. With him is under his.

We need supportive complementary Co-Leadership and Relational Mutual Accountability (iron sharpening iron) in decision making. He knows, has always known and always will know what would be in our own benefit and best for the big picture – but *Love never demands its own way.* We do not know, we suppose – as we *lean on our own understanding*. In Authority, we think that we may banish others from our gardens (as God did) due to their disobedience. But we are not God, and Jesus never banished either. He beckoned. He told people:

Come to me. My yoke is easy, my burden light.

He did not burden people. He never sent anyone away from his presence, and he never threatened that he *might* send them away from his presence if they did not align and submit fully to his Direction. On the contrary, they failed him frequently and he kept right on living with them. Many left him, but he never cast anyone away from his presence.

We may utilize his Unity OS similarly, and at the same time allow for Self-Selection, as he does. In the *Life* section we related that, in a sense, God did not kick out Adam and Eve. He gave them the information they needed beforehand and allowed them to decide what they wanted to do. They were the ones who decided that the risk of death was worth what the Enemy promised they would gain. And so it was that, in a sense, *they Self-Selected* to leave God and instead followed his Enemy out into the world.

When we provide Unity Operating System clarity at the inception of every team, business, organization or entity, new team members will have *agreed* to the "terms" of our Values before they join us. Having had this discussion in advance it would be fair to point to it later if behavioral issues occur. Then, if the behavior continues in some way, have the type of conversation with them that we would expect of God.

"Tom, as we agreed before we came together to accomplish our mutual goals in Unity, the type of behavior you are engaging in now is not acceptable. We agreed about the need for Unity behavior from the very start. Are you Self-Selecting out? We would love to have you stay and collaborate synergistically, but your behavior is often divisive. If you want to continue in that behavior, you know you can't do it here. If that is the case, we'd love to have you back some day if you ever change your mind. Please help us understand if there is something else going on, but right now it looks to us like you are Self-Selecting your way out. Is that right?"

Though the very real result of departing from Jesus could/would mean separation from him forever – he graciously let them choose for themselves. They could return or remain separated, but he would not apply even the slightest amount of *man*ipulation or coercion to help them make the right decision – for their own benefit.

His way is to hold us close, though loosely, sincerely inviting us to stay while allowing us to leave.

Malachi 3:6-7a

6 "For I the Lord do not change; therefore you, O children of Jacob, are not consumed. 7 From the days of your fathers you have turned aside from my statutes and have not kept them. Return to me, and I will return to you, says the Lord of hosts. But you say, 'How shall we return?'

James 4:1-12

1 What causes quarrels and what causes fights among you? Is it not this, that your passions are at war within you? 2 You desire and do not have, so you murder. You covet and cannot obtain, so you fight and quarrel. You do not have, because you do not ask. 3 You ask and do not receive, because you ask wrongly, to spend it on your passions. 4 You adulterous people! Do you not know that friendship with the world is enmity with God? Therefore whoever wishes to be a friend of the world makes himself an enemy of God. 5 Or do you suppose it is to no purpose that the Scripture says, "He yearns jealously over the spirit that he has made to dwell in us"? 6 But he gives more grace. Therefore it says, "God opposes the proud but gives grace to the humble." 7 Submit yourselves therefore to God. Resist the devil, and he will flee from you. 8 Draw near to God, and he will draw near to you.

In the Military Chain of Command we have rules. In government they are called laws. In the Spirit of the Lord there is freedom (2 Corinthians 3:17). Therefore, in the Family of God, we have agreements and disagreements which may continue to be clarified over time. As we are conformed into God's image - *collectively* - iron sharpens iron *Respectfully* and *Relationally*, desirous of the *collective wisdom* he provides us for greater productivity in *Unity*.

There is a big difference between Rules and Agreements. The saying "Rules are made to be broken." emanates from a lack of respect for the rule maker(s) due to disagreement about "the rule", which therefore ignites our emotion to rebel against Authoritarian Control.

Agreements, on the other hand, are freely made *together*, are understood by each, have a level of respect for the *relationship* that exists between the agreeing parties, and ignite the sense of loyalty and integrity that lead *us* to follow through on the agreement.

Rules are made to be broken, so the Ruler will always have rebels. But agreements are *Relational* commitments *to each other*. As iron sharpens iron, agreements may be revised. Rules, however, are rigid and beg rebellion because they are Controlling, and nobody wants to be Controlled. All want their say in the matter, but Rulers don't care about that. They just want their way. But God continually shows up with a warning to Controlling tyrants, and to call his people out of the slavery of the Controllers. From cover to cover, the bible is clear.

Exodus 8:1
Then the Lord said to Moses, "Go in to Pharaoh and say to him, 'Thus says the Lord, "Let my people go, that they may serve me.

1 Samuel 8:6
But the thing displeased Samuel when they said, "Give us a king to judge us." And Samuel prayed to the Lord.

Hosea 13:9-12
9 He destroys you, O Israel, for you are against me, against your helper.
10 Where now is your king, to save you in all your cities? Where are all your rulers - those of whom you said, "Give me a king and princes"?
11 I gave you a king in my anger, and I took him away in my wrath.
12 The iniquity of Ephraim is bound up; his sin is kept in store.

Mark 10:42-45
42 And Jesus called them to him and said to them, "You know that those
who are considered rulers of the Gentiles lord it over them, and their great
ones exercise authority over them. 43 But it shall not be so among you. But
whoever would be great among you must be your servant, 44 and whoever
would be first among you must be slave of all. 45 For even the Son of Man
came not to be served but to serve, and to give his life
as a ransom for many."

Revelation 22:10-13
10 And he said to me, "Do not seal up the words of the prophecy of this
book, for the time is near. 11 Let the evildoer still do evil, and the filthy still
be filthy, and the righteous still do right, and the holy still be holy."
12 "Behold, I am coming soon, bringing my recompense with me, to repay
each one for what he has done. 13 I am the Alpha and the Omega, the first
and the last, the beginning and the end."

Chapter Ten

Relational Mutual Accountability

Proverbs 27:17
Iron sharpens iron, and one man sharpens another.

Relational Mutual Accountability: Iron Sharpening Iron
Most of us focus more upon leadership *or* discipleship than we do leadership *and* discipleship. The two go hand-in-hand, yet most organizations neglect one or the other. As you may have guessed, Directors operating under Individuated Authority tend more toward leadership development and Reconcilers operating under Individuated Authority tend more toward disciple development. We see them occurring in tandem only where balanced D+R leadership has been operating.

Business HR departments tend to use phrases like "socialize into our culture" rather than "disciple", but whatever term Christ Following Leaders use, it is to be toward use of the Unity OS.

At issue is the World OS cultural value that training from leaders not be questioned. That is, since they are "in Control" we must learn, follow and adopt "their" system. But that is unwise. In this way our leaders are somewhat to mostly unaccountable themselves – and situationally we end up following *them* instead of *him*.

Whether an Individuated Director or an Individuated Reconciler, the individuated operator uses Hierarchy, Power, Authority and Leverage to accomplish their goals. Authority includes subtle and not so subtle "do this or else" statements that threaten. Because "Somebody has to be the boss and it happens to be me – so fall in line." But even God does not do that.

God's ways are not our ways. Love never Demands its own way. Love is Patient. Love is Kind. Adonai, the Triune God, moves in unison, though we mostly move at the direction of individuals. I have seen corporate boards and elder/council-led organizations vote in Unity when in reality it was a rubber stamp from a stacked court weighted toward Directors or Reconcilers.

Whether a business, church or Non-Profit/NGO, Directors require Reconcilers. Reconcilers require Directors. Groups of Teams and Teams of Groups balanced with Directors and Reconcilers lead better than one Director and one Reconciler. Directors and Reconcilers are nothing without the support of Active Implementers. Allowing ALL of the information into deliberations as iron is allowed to sharpen iron is a talent of discipline that no individual can sustain alone.

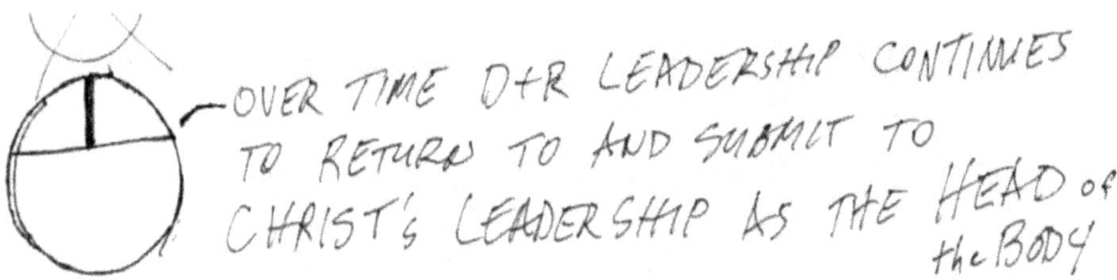

Talmidim mature as each are willing to continually train and be trained. We are never so far along that we can handle individuated directing. Look for discipline. Seek out Wisdom. Loving, Patient and Kind. Especially in disagreement.

Proverbs 4:5-6

5 Get wisdom; get insight; do not forget, and do not turn away from the words of my mouth. 6 Do not forsake her, and she will keep you; love her, and she will guard you.

Proverbs 18:15

An intelligent heart acquires knowledge,
and the ear of the wise seeks knowledge.

Proverbs 17:17

A friend loves at all times, and a brother is born for adversity.

When Director+Reconciler Co-Leadership fails, it is usually because the Director has worn down the Reconciler over time. Little by little, strong Directors with the best of intentions usurp control from their Reconcilers. (Who can blame our Directors and why should we be surprised? From childhood they were trained in the ways of the World OS of Individuated Leadership and the use of Hierarchy, Power, Authority and Leverage.) The strong overcome. The cream rises to the top. Take the mantle. Seize the day. This is simply what we do!

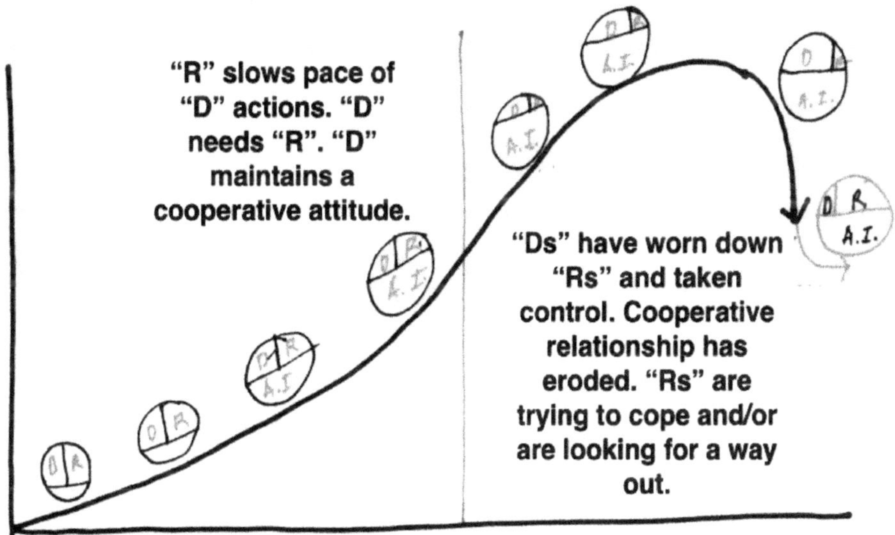

Cultural training in the hierarchical World OS tells Reconcilers to let Directors usurp control. In addition, Directors typically have tremendous energy and are able to press on long after others have tired. As Directors develop trust initially, and as Reconcilers find that an acquiescence here or there was without consequence, the tendency of the Director is to push for more latitude. Unfortunately, it is the beginning of the end since these bursts of freedom also allow Directors to place additional Directors around themselves in support and gain greater Leverage for future considerations.

The key to the sustainability of D+R relationships is an unwavering commitment to his Unity At All Cost values. As Leader Multiplication occurs, it is necessary that each do the same – with supportive facilitation and Relational Mutual Accountability among all.

We are committed to:

- One-ness: Him in us and us in Him
- Acts of Love & Intercession
- Hearts after the Father in attitudes consistent with the Beatitudes: Jesus' attitudes
- Fruit of the Spirit Language & Actions
- Connecting & Inviting
- Relational Mutually Accountable Co-Discipleship

- Development of Balanced Director/Reconciler Teams in Co-Leadership
- Leadership Teams that Do Not Have or Use Hierarchy/Authority
- Unity/Unanimity in Decisions & Actions
- Groups of Teams and Teams of Groups
- Leadership Development at All Levels
- Advisory Forums at ALL levels
    - *Collective* discernment of the Input of ALL People
    - Has God brought us a Leader Out Of Nowhere, now here?
- Facilitating Spirit-Led Self-Selection of Service

We do a disservice to our alpha Directors when we allow their competency strengths to cause us to overlook their Reconciler immaturity. We do a disservice to our alpha Reconcilers when we allow their competency strengths to cause us to overlook their Director immaturity. Our lack of willingness to Persevere in Patience and Peace with Kind and Gentle correction diminishes their growth opportunity - even though productivity is greater in the one case and relational Unity greater in the other.

It is not suggested that hiring be type dependent. However, we do need an awareness of type tendencies and preferences such that ongoing growth and development may occasionally be rebalanced. In this way, the complementary inclusion and integration of Director and Reconciler differences is continually reviewed. As integration continues, they help each other strengthen, build up and bring balance to one another's individual Director/Reconciler/Active Implementer selves.

It is important to mention that I have witnessed marvelously balanced Senior Pastors in hierarchical organizational structures who rejected the temptation to take control and lead as CEO. Rejecting Hierarchy & Authority, these pastors created co-leadership systems which established the "We are committed to:" values listed above within the hierarchical structure they inherited. They clearly understand what it means to be *collectively* committed to Christ the Head, doing the will of the Father as he does his works in us, by the leading of the Holy Spirit.

If you are in a hierarchical situation, it may be wise to do as these pastors did first. Then, having modelled collective leadership, persuade for the formal abolishment of that structure into the flat one where ALL are on the SAME organizational level, with Christ the only Head.

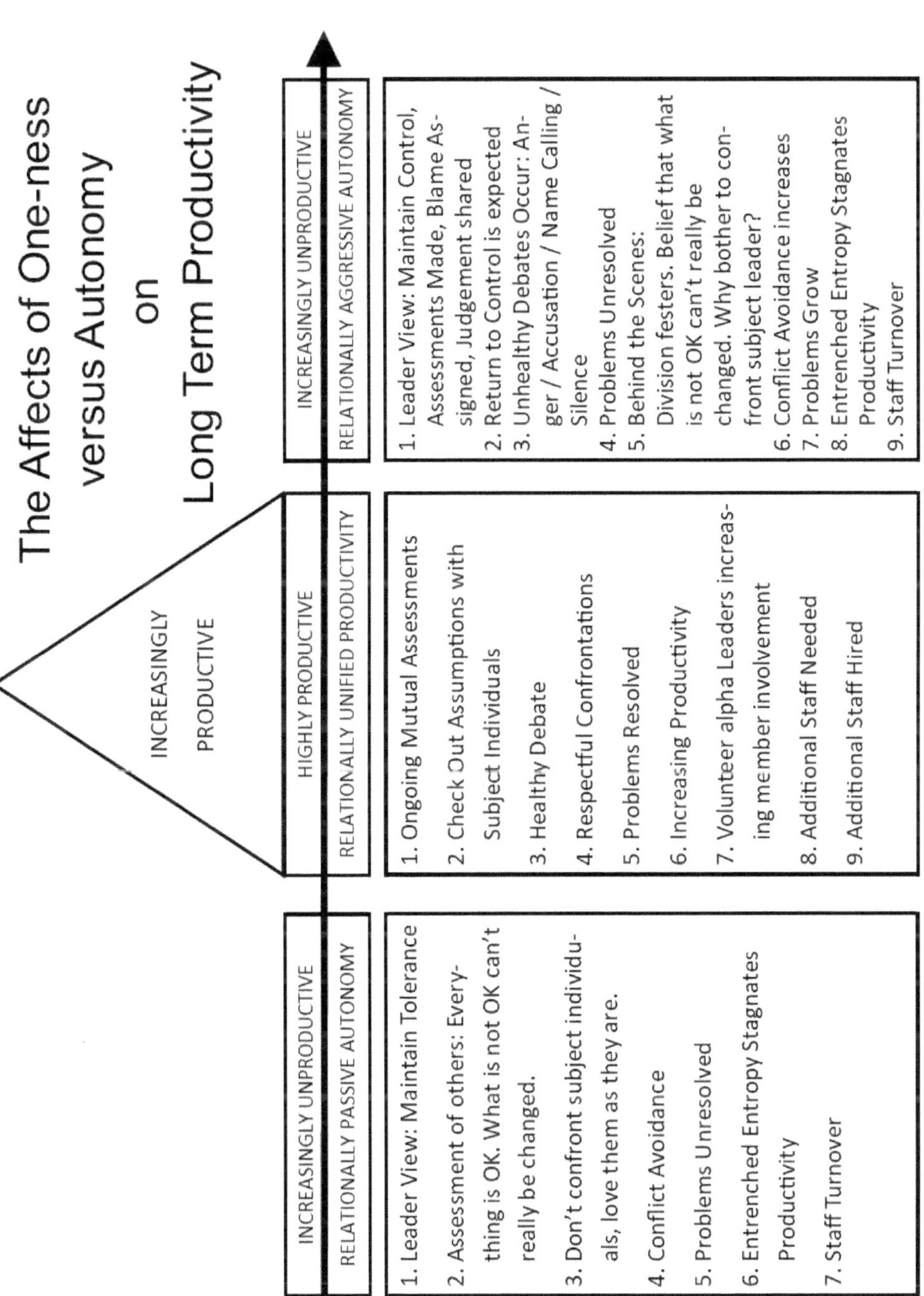

Chapter Eleven

Leadership Vacillations

Common vacillations of the Senior Pastor led church over long periods of time:

Reconciler Senior Pastors are typically challenged by Director congregation members to be more productive. Over time Director type congregation members wear down the council/board/elders and receive some degree of accommodation. This may be followed by the Reconciler Senior Pastor leaving the church in rejection of such conflict and disunity.

The opposite happens when the Director Senior Pastor is challenged by congregation member Reconcilers to be more relational. Over time Reconciler type congregation members wear down the council/board/elders and get some degree of accommodation. This may be followed by the Director Senior Pastor leaving the church in rejection of his loss of autonomy and a sense that "they just don't get it" – while Reconciler church members note the relational damage done and say, "He/she just didn't get it!"

If you ask older congregation members to describe what has transpired in the way of the several Senior Pastors they have had during the course of their 50 year membership, you will often find the following teeter-tottering back and forth to have occurred.

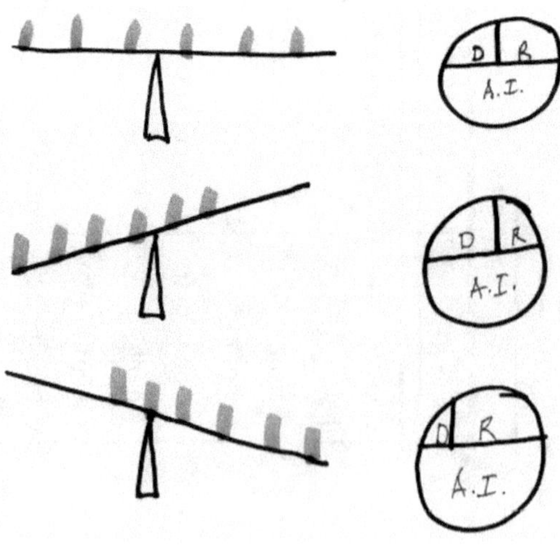

Take care here, just because the same Senior Pastor has been in place for 20-30-40 years, it does not mean that all is well! Sometimes an Individuated Director or an Individuated Reconciler can survive decades without any significant challenge. The situations we described in the paragraphs above assumed congregation members *stayed* and *challenged* the thinking of the overbearing Director or unproductive Reconciler. But what if they leave rather than challenge? Leader Replication will occur such that the entire congregation will look more and more like the Senior Pastor:

When out-of-balance councils/elders/boards hire a Senior Pastor, the likely result is a hire that looks like they do. In these cases, Leader Replication starts with them. Over time, their Director or Reconciler Senior Pastor choice will easily be able to hire more staff members like themselves, and their broadly United front will become increasingly more difficult for congregation members to penetrate in Mutual Accountability. When congregation members leave rather than challenge, the congregation itself begins to look more and more like their Lead Leaders – and goes further and further out of balance.

While in the beginning it is simply a matter of uncomfortable conflict or wasted potential, over time it may easily grow extremely harmful. You won't have to think very long to remember some with national disgrace, some that were cultish (including mass suicides) and others with sermons asking God to damn America. It is highly unlikely that they started out that way, and far more likely that they regressed over time. These remind me of my friend, mentioned in the *Life* section, who was slowly indoctrinated into a local "church" that mind Controlled him and sexually Abused him. These dangers are real and of great consequence, but they often start small!

Co-Led, Co-Taught, Relationally Accountable

As was described in detail in *Life*, in Jesus' day, a lone rabbi teaching in a synagogue was unusual. Rather, all of the rabbis from the insulas in the area (often five or more rabbis with hundreds of people in attendance) would gather in the synagogue to *conversationally* consider the appointed text of that sabbath day. *The people* were allowed to ask questions and weigh in on these discussions conversationally as well.

With several rabbis present, no one rabbi could steer the people in an unhealthy direction over time. In *conversational* style, God could send in his *Encouragers*, *Disruptors* and *Correctors* to contribute to the discussions and raise up issues and scripture for community deliberation. It was this setup that made it possible for Jesus to speak *in any synagogue on any sabbath*.

Personally involved, please note that history identifies that most of the people in these communities had *thoroughly memorized* their Torah. Knowing that they could engage their teachers, stimulating thoughts and memorable discussion on the related texts could facilitate the deeper contemplations that lead to changed lives. The lone teacher setup is a heady situation that risks the people *becoming* teacher followers rather than talmidim of *Jesus*.

We would do well to reconsider our tradition of individuals teaching to gatherings by lecture. Rather, let's afford people conversational iron sharpening iron opportunities. Our only requirement should be that they do so with hearts after the Father, humbly postured in the attitudes of the Beatitudes, and that they share thoughts in true fruit of the Spirit language and actions. If we will do so, we just might see our communities begin to flourish once again.

The USA as a Nation: Made in God's Triune Image

We have no record to indicate that they recognized it as such, but the framers used Adonai's One-ness in setting up a Godly Governmental Structure in the United States of America.

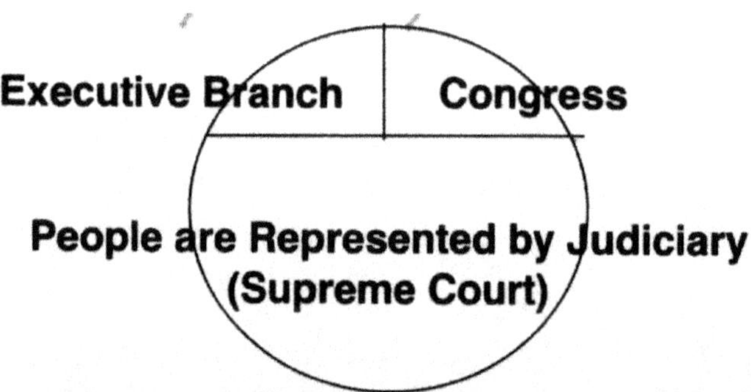

The Executive Branch is representative of the Directors, the Congress is representative of the Reconcilers and the Judiciary is representative of the Active Implementers. In this way the President and his Cabinet in the Executive Branch lead in direction, Congress attempts to reconcile their position to that direction (making laws that they believe will be good for all people) and the Judiciary provides the counterbalance (through the Supreme

Court) should the Executive Branch and the Congress act separately rather than in Unity.

It is important to note that the people have not given over Authority to either the Executive Branch or Congress. Rather, they have elected "elders" whom they believe will best represent all of the people in Unity - while themselves being represented by the Judiciary - with the understanding that all people should Actively Support Implementation of the Unified decisions these duly elected leaders make on their behalf.

It all works well when our House, Senate and President are United in Relational Mutual Accountability (iron sharpening iron) & Co-Leadership - as has been the case for much of the USA's 200+ years. As with any organization, however, it all falls apart when we operate in disrespectful defiance of each other. In recent history we have been bouncing back and forth between Director Democrats and Director Republicans trying to take the upper hand (Who can blame them? After all, that is how the World OS trained them!) as the minority of elected Reconcilers try to bring collaboration and balance.

From time to time we have seen the good and the bad of Director/Reconciler defiance, both in the USA and the world. Here are some notable examples:

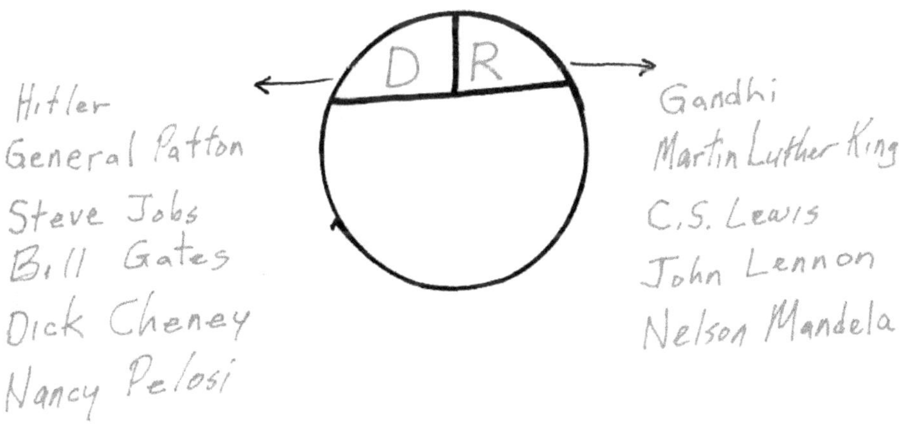

For quite some time now, we have been experiencing the damage caused when we lose sight of our Unity values. Our (Director) Presidents have been taking Executive Action beyond that with which our (Reconciler) Congress can agree. They have each been taking actions in defiance of the other and the (Active Implementer) Supreme Court has been representing the (Active Implementer) People to (hopefully) bring that Reconciliation about.

It's not pretty, and we see that they are not working together according to the values of God's Unity Operating System, but that is not the fault of his Unity OS. In fact, a case may easily be made that his System and Structure *are* working quite well in that we are in a period of immobility while the Unity is being worked out. (Though some are trying to change the Constitutional Structure so that they might seize and retain Control indefinitely.)

Fortunately and unfortunately, it is now up to the Active Implementers to make changes to these Director/Reconciler relationships in the coming elections. Unity is a slow and sometimes tedious process, but I have faith that God is actively working in the lives of his Active Implementer people to bring greater Unity about. We The People have voted the Corrupt into office. Now, if we will return to Godly Triune Government, we must be the ones to vote them out.

One of the hopes I have for this book is that we will come to a place of better understanding Relationally that helps us to re-commit as a country to following in his ways and ending the Foolishness. Please ask of God that his kingdom would come and his will would be done in our elections, that his will be done on earth as it is in heaven.

If anything is to change, you must do your part in your sphere of influence. Our politicos are working hard at making kings of themselves, and We The People are responsible for that - because we keep voting them back in.

1 Samuel 8:7-9

7 And the Lord said to Samuel, "Obey the voice of the people in all that they say to you, for they have not rejected you, but they have rejected me from being king over them. 8 According to all the deeds that they have done, from the day I brought them up out of Egypt even to this day, forsaking me and serving other gods, so they are also doing to you. 9 Now then, obey their voice; only you shall solemnly warn them and show them the ways of the king who shall reign over them."

Please persist (as did the Persistent Widow in Luke 18) in asking for justice against our adversaries, in praying *for* our enemies, and for the sending of laborers to the Fools and those Corrupted by Evil. That they might turn, repent, and follow God all the days of their lives. Otherwise, that he replace them with the Wise.

It is so common these days to seek the power and Authority to control outcomes: personally, corporately and in governance. Even his disciples were tempted:

Mark 9:33-35

33 And they came to Capernaum. And when he was in the house he asked them, "What were you discussing on the way?" 34 But they kept silent, for on the way they had argued with one another about who was the greatest. 35 And he sat down and called the twelve. And he said to them, "If anyone would be first, he must be last of all and servant of all."

Who was greatest among them could only have been important in the determination of who had the most power, and therefore the ability to use it. If I am greater than you then you need to follow my lead – and I will be in Control. The time has come to return once again:

Hosea 12:2, 5-6

2 The Lord has an indictment against Judah and will punish Jacob according to his ways; he will repay him according to his deeds. 5 the Lord, the God of hosts, the Lord is his memorial name: 6 "So you, by the help of your God, return, hold fast to love and justice,
and wait continually for your God."

Otherwise:

Hosea 12:8-11, 14

8 Ephraim has said, "Ah, but I am rich; I have found wealth for myself; in all my labors they cannot find in me iniquity or sin." 9 I am the Lord your God
from the land of Egypt; I will again make you dwell in tents, as in the days of the appointed feast. 10 I spoke to the prophets; it was I who multiplied visions, and through the prophets gave parables. 11 If there is iniquity in Gilead, they shall surely come to nothing: in Gilgal they sacrifice bulls; their altars also are like stone heaps on the furrows of the field.

14 Ephraim has given bitter provocation; so his Lord will leave his bloodguilt on him and will repay him for his disgraceful deeds.

Job 19:7

Behold, I cry out, 'Violence!' but I am not answered;
I call for help, but there is no justice.

Hosea 13:9-12

9 He destroys you, O Israel, for you are against me, against your helper.
10 Where now is your king, to save you in all your cities? Where are all your
rulers - those of whom you said, "Give me a king and princes"? 11 I gave
you a king in my anger, and I took him away in my wrath. 12 The iniquity of
Ephraim is bound up; his sin is kept in store.

The framers, led by God, set the foundation of this nation on God alone. The United States Constitution is a God-led document for Godly Governance, the first of its kind in the entire world. Over the last sixty years, though, the Enemy has succeeded in entrenching the Corrupt and multiplying their presence in our institutions, and since they have taken Control, we have been tearing down the USA precept by precept. "So you, by the help of your God, *return*, hold fast to love and justice, and wait continually for your God." Hosea 12:6.

Psalm 127:1

Unless the Lord builds the house, those who build it labor in vain. Unless the Lord watches over the city, the watchman stays awake in vain.

City and County (Regional) Government

To look at his structure considering changing scale, we need only remind ourselves that our state and local governments work (or don't work) under the very same structure, and that we as individuals and families do so as well.

Mayors & Cty Board Chair
Councils & Boards
People are Represented by Judiciary

Families

Husband
& Wife
Children

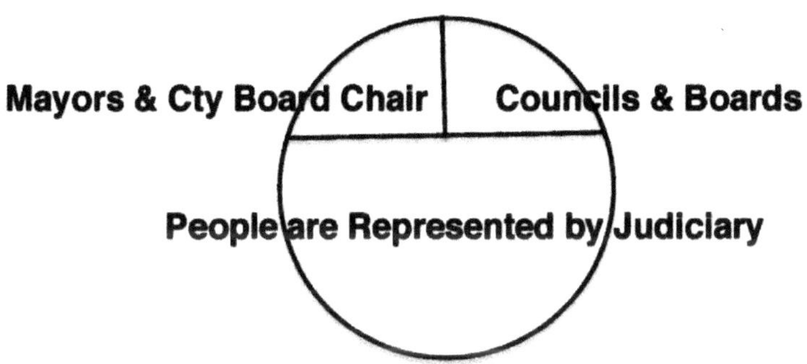

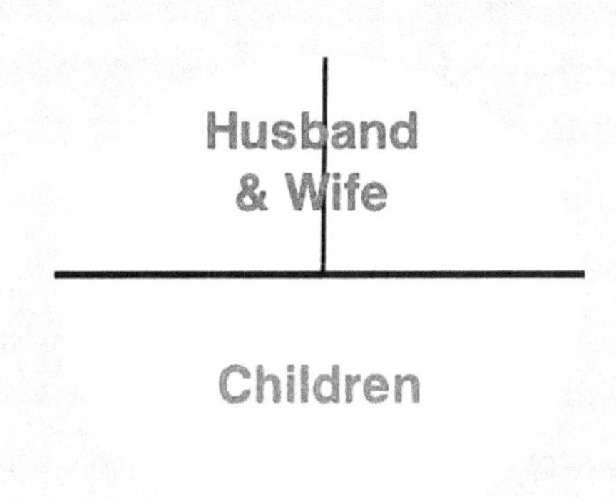

Chapter Twelve

Working With Alphas

Before we can scale up using the Unity Operating System and Structure, we will need to be confident that we can sustain it in our basic relationships – how frequently I see that we do not! The Authority culture is always beckoning us back, and surrounded by it every day, we are at risk continuously. Like the addicted, we need to become keenly aware of its allure if we will sustain God's way. Paul understood the allure:

Philippians 3

1 Finally, my brothers, rejoice in the Lord. To write the same things to you is no trouble to me and is safe for you. 2 Look out for the dogs, look out for the evildoers, look out for those who mutilate the flesh. 3 For we are the circumcision, who worship by the Spirit of God and glory in Christ Jesus and put no confidence in the flesh— 4 though I myself have reason for confidence in the flesh also. If anyone else thinks he has reason for confidence in the flesh, I have more: 5 circumcised on the eighth day, of the people of Israel, of the tribe of Benjamin, a Hebrew of Hebrews; as to the law, a Pharisee; 6 as to zeal, a persecutor of the church; as to righteousness under the law, blameless. 7 But whatever gain I had, I counted as loss for the sake of Christ. 8 Indeed, I count everything as loss because of the surpassing worth of knowing Christ Jesus my Lord. For his sake I have suffered the loss of all things and count them as rubbish, in order that I may gain Christ 9 and be found in him, not having a righteousness of my own that comes from the law, but that which comes through faith in Christ, the righteousness from God that depends on faith— 10 that I may know him and the power of his resurrection, and may share his sufferings, becoming like him in his death, 11 that by any means possible I may attain the resurrection from the dead. 12 Not that I have already obtained this or am already perfect, but I press on to make it my own, because Christ Jesus has made me his own. 13 Brothers, I do not consider that I have made it my own. But one thing I do: forgetting what lies behind and straining forward to what lies ahead, 14 I press on toward the goal for the prize of the upward call of God in Christ Jesus. 15 Let those of us who are mature think this way, and if

<u>in anything you think otherwise, God will reveal that also to you</u>. 16 <u>Only let us hold true to what we have attained.</u> 17 Brothers, join in imitating me, and keep your eyes on those who walk according to the example you have in us. 18 For <u>many</u>, of whom I have often told you and now tell you even with tears, <u>walk as enemies of the cross of Christ.</u> 19 <u>Their end is destruction, their god is their belly, and they glory in their shame, with minds set on earthly things</u>. 20 But our citizenship is in heaven, and from it we await a Savior, the Lord Jesus Christ, 21 who will transform our lowly body to be like his glorious body, by the power that enables him even to subject all things to himself.

3 John 9-10 NIV

9 I wrote to the church, but Diotrephes, <u>who loves to be first</u>, will not welcome us. 10 So when I come, I will call attention to what he is doing, spreading malicious nonsense about us. Not satisfied with that, he even refuses to welcome other believers. He also stops those who want to do so and puts them out of the church.

There is a popular phrase being used these days by leaders who have moved in the direction of collective leadership, but who do not want to fully comply: *First among equals*.

They say, "Sometimes somebody just needs to take charge and make a decision when none seems forthcoming in consensus." This is a very dangerous precedent that moves us back toward Authoritarian leadership. The process of such a corruption is well spelled out in George Orwell's book <u>Animal Farm</u>. As they left Authoritarian leadership in favor of collective leadership, the corrupting influence of power eventually led to this leader statement: "All animals are equal, but some animals are more equal than others." As they became "First Among Equals", they returned the farm to a state worse than what they had before.

You and Your Alphas

If you are a leader of leaders, you are likely an alpha. If so, God saved you, an alpha, from yourself: the know-it-all you; the stubborn you; the proud you; the domineering you; the skeptical you; the critical you; the overbearing you; the cynical you; the closed-minded you; the bossy you. He is continuing his sanctification of you. You are worth it – and so are his other alphas:

Titus 3:3-8

3 For we ourselves were once foolish, disobedient, led astray, slaves to various passions and pleasures, passing our days in malice and envy, hated by others and hating one another. 4 But when the goodness and loving kindness of God our Savior appeared, 5 he saved us, not because of works done by us in righteousness, but according to his own mercy, by the washing of regeneration and renewal of the Holy Spirit, 6 whom he poured out on us richly through Jesus Christ our Savior, 7 so that being justified by his grace we might become heirs according to the hope of eternal life. 8 The saying is trustworthy, and I want you to insist on these things, so that those who have believed in God may be careful to devote themselves to good works. These things are excellent and profitable for people.

God doesn't *need* you to do good works. He loves you and has invited you to be one of his willing talmidim in the Joy of *creative collaboration* with him – not co-leadership. *He* is Directing *you*, and you are attempting to Reconcile your position to his. He made a Connection with you. He has Advised (and sometimes commanded) you. He is giving you every opportunity to become One with him, though your ways are not his ways. Your passion, giftedness and call have been given for a purpose. One-ness is his purpose for all of us - including the other alphas - together.

The above paragraph summarizes *how God offers participation to us*. I believe it follows that we could similarly summarize what collaboration looks like *with those who might join us* in him:

We need everyone. We will do our best to love you like he loves you. He has invited you to be one of his talmidim and since you are here, we will engage in it with you. We are confident that it includes both Co-Leadership and Co-Discipleship in Relational Mutual Accountability. He is Directing you, and you are attempting to Reconcile your position to his. So are we. He made a Connection with you and a Connection has been initiated with us. He has Advised (and sometimes commanded) you as he has also done with us that we would love him and love others, not leaning on our own understanding. He is giving us every opportunity to become One with him, through him in us. Though his ways are not our ways, we will try to learn his ways for us. Your passion, giftedness and sense of call have been given for a purpose and we will engage with you to learn how we fit together as his Body, remembering that Christ is the Head, that collectively we may better discern the mind of Christ and therefore better accomplish his will for us together. One-ness is his purpose for all of us, and then together to serve the world around us. We promise to engage with you in that order, never allowing a productivity focus to damage our desire for Mutually Accountable relational Unity.

He told us to go make talmidim even while we are still being sanctified ourselves. Not being Jesus, our discipleship of others is often wanting. We cannot teach what we do not understand. Unfortunately, because most of us have been Deceived into using the Authoritarian World OS, we have blocked out one of God's best ways *of* discipleship for us as alphas: Relational Mutually Accountable Co-Discipleship.

God says: None better than another. None with Authority over another. Ongoing sanctification as iron sharpens iron. Each with the potential for Co-Leadership.

Our Adversary says, "Look at his failings. He is a risk! You have the responsibility! Somebody *has* to be the boss and you're it. He is too stubborn. He is a dangerous leader, he will not submit to your leadership (Authority & responsibility)."

Then we remember that we have an out in what God continues on to say to us in Titus:

Titus 3:10-11

10 As for a person who stirs up division, after warning him once and then twice, <u>have nothing more to do with him</u>, 11 knowing that such a person is warped and sinful; he is self-condemned.

The Enemy wants you to quit on your alphas.
He is always there telling us that we do not have time for this stuff!

God, though, <u>wants</u> you to take the time for Mutually Accountable Relational Co-Discipleship with them. In fact, as he told Peter, forgive them seventy-seven times, and, "just as I have loved you, you also are to love one another. By this all people will know that you are my talmidim, if you have love for one another."

Peter was opinionated not divisive, and passionate - like most of our alphas. We just think they are divisive because they are not submitting to (or maybe not acknowledging of) our *hierarchical position* of Authority and the respect that we believe we are entitled to by virtue *of* that position.

This is a syllogism and FAE that may only be supported by the premise of Authority.

In the ways of the world there can only be one boss, so we rarely "warn" in a truly two-way dialogue where we must also listen. We just Judge them and then avoid them because we don't have a proper understanding – and it is much, much easier than a relationship with a "Peter". Our side of this is that we think we get to decide by the Authority and responsibilities of leadership. Their side is that they want to bring Correction to our error. Our assumptions allow us to rationalize separation and cause us to lose the synergy we could have otherwise gained.

1 Corinthians 12:21-27
21 The eye cannot say to the hand, "I have no need of you," nor again the head to the feet, "I have no need of you." 22 On the contrary, the parts of the body that seem to be weaker are indispensable, 23 and on those parts of the body that we think less honorable we bestow the greater honor, and our unpresentable parts are treated with greater modesty, 24 which our more presentable parts do not require. But God has so composed the body, giving greater honor to the part that lacked it, 25 <u>that there may be no division in the body, but that the members may have the same care for one another</u>. 26 If one member suffers, all suffer together; if one member is honored, all rejoice together. 27 Now you are the body of Christ and individually members of it.

God plays the "long game" with us. We like to cut to the chase and *"have nothing more to do with him"* because we think we don't have the time for the "difficult" alphas that God has for us. Do not let your insights, knowledge and understandings cause you to Rationalize for Avoidance. If we will Persevere in Patience, Gentleness, Kindness, Goodness and Self-Control in fruit of the Spirit language, we just may find Peace that surpasses all understanding with a new willing partner. Learning more and more how to Love, we also find Joy.

1 Corinthians 13:1-3
1 If I speak in the tongues of men and of angels, but have not love, I am a noisy gong or a clanging cymbal. 2 And if I have prophetic powers, and understand all mysteries and all knowledge, and if I have all faith, so as to remove mountains, but have not love, I am nothing. 3 If I give away all I have, and if I deliver up my body to be burned, but have not love, I gain nothing.

Love your alphas, too.

1 Corinthians 13:4-7
4 Love is patient and kind; love does not envy or boast; it is not arrogant 5 or rude. It does not insist on its own way; it is not irritable or resentful; 6 it does not rejoice at wrongdoing, but rejoices with the truth. 7 Love bears all things, believes all things, hopes all things, endures all things.

I cannot know all things, so God brings me help in the form of people and information. My help is in the name of the Lord, and many are passionate alphas. The Enemy tries to separate us by convincing us to ignore strong-willed alphas. But they know some things we do not know, and we need all of the perspectives we can get.

1 Corinthians 13:8-13 NIV
8 Love never fails. But where there are prophecies, they will cease; where there are tongues, they will be stilled; where there is knowledge, it will pass away. 9 <u>For we know in part and we prophesy in part,</u> 10 but when completeness comes, what is in part disappears. 11 When I was a child, I talked like a child, I thought like a child, I reasoned like a child. When I became a man, I put the ways of childhood behind me. 12 <u>For now we see only a reflection as in a mirror; then we shall see face to face. Now I know in part;</u> then I shall know fully, even as I am fully known. 13 And now these three remain: faith, hope and love. But the greatest of these is love.

It's just like high school. (There are alphas in action around you.)
When I was in high school I thought like a high schooler. When I became a Christ Follower, I gave up my high schooler ways.

Only now the stakes are higher. This isn't a football game, high school sweetheart or popularity contest we're talking about, it's Adonai - and the Lost. Ours cannot be a competition about who is right. There are eternal consequences. It's our utmost for his highest. Lives are on the line. This is war of the spiritual kind, and the Enemy knows it better than us.

If we want to win, we will only have a chance if we make God's ways our ways. His ways are Unity first, inclusive and transparent. The Enemy's way is to divide and conquer and block transparency - and that is what he wants between alphas – Division. Alpha synergy is a great risk to his schemes, so he tells us that *we* are the one with the title of Pastor, Teacher, Apostle, Prophet, Evangelist, Senior Pastor, CEO Pastor, or COO Pastor, and that *the office* and the responsibilities *of* that office are *ours* - so *they* need to recognize that and back off. But God has warned us that these are not to be our ways. For if they are, they will tempt us toward separation, isolation and individuation.

Though over the years I have been called Pastor, Teacher, Apostle, Prophet and Evangelist out of respect, I have always asked to be called only by my name. Otherwise, I will be tempted to use that title for my personal benefit.

Matthew 23:8-12
8 But you are not to be called rabbi, for you have one teacher, and you
are all brothers. 9 And call no man your father on earth, for you have one
Father, who is in heaven. 10 Neither be called instructors, for you have one
instructor, the Christ. 11 The greatest among you shall be your
servant. 12 Whoever exalts himself will be humbled,
and whoever humbles himself will be exalted.

The only instances of a capital letter at the front of the words pastor, teacher, apostle, prophet or evangelist in the Bible refer to Jesus. When did we decide that we should call them offices or positions and include capital letters as was only done for the Christ? Pastor, Teacher, Apostle, Prophet, Evangelist, Senior Pastor, CEO Pastor, COO Pastor, Reverend, Dr., MDiv, Deacon, etc. The Bible will say that Paul was an apostle and Elijah a prophet, but there are no capital letters calling them Apostle Paul or Prophet Elijah. Shall we elevate ourselves above them?

There is nothing wrong with identifying Body Parts structurally as long as they are simply categories such as teaching pastor, deacon, youth pastor, outreach leader, etc.

Otherwise, the additional danger in the use of *titles and offices* is that the congregants within our sphere of influence, living in a *world* of titles and Authority, will begin to lift us up *over* them. This is a very heady situation in which, having been placed above them *by them*, we just might accept their adulations and slide back into functioning with Leverage and Hierarchically. After all, it is what folks with these trainings expect of us!

****

We are failing together – subtly. We compete, debate, posture, suppress, rationalize, minimize, triangulate. Eyes don't see, ears don't hear. When two alphas meet to discuss a topic of mutual interest what happens? Positional circumstances determine if one holds the upper hand, and if so, they will expect to keep it (Authoritarian posture). Whoever thinks they have the greater experience will posture to imply that. Each will *MAN*euver to maintain or improve their position – just as the apostles were doing that day.

What if one of these alphas is the Individuated Senior Pastor of the church the other attends? What are the tendencies? What is the likelihood for a Unified conclusion? Similar in giftedness, similar in intellect, similar in capacity, differing in experience and with thousands of years of culture teaching us that there can only be one boss – it is likely that there will be posturing. "I am the Pastor." It is what is done. But God's way is better.

When we are mature, balanced and United with him in our hearts, souls and minds, we may more effectively communicate. Practice utilizing *fruit of the Spirit* language and actions that you more and more *become* a talmid of Jesus, and therefore a more effective communicator doing the will of the Father. Kindly, Gently, Perseveringly, Peaceably and with Goodness. As we learn to live with hearts after the Father and in the attitudes of the Beatitudes, this posture and humility will prepare us for fruit of the Spirit language and actions in each and every interaction.

We must learn his ways of Relational Mutual Accountability in Co-Discipleship if we will sustainably Connect our alpha brothers and sisters to The Body. As was described in the *Life* section, It might accurately be said that the depth of our trust and understanding will bring us to the depth of our faith. And that the depth of our love is based upon these. Develop trust with your alphas in Mutual Accountability and Co-Discipleship - and then watch God work.

His ways are Unity first, inclusive and transparent. The Enemy's way is to divide and conquer and block transparency - and that is what he wants between alphas – Division. Alpha synergy is a great risk to his schemes.

****

Unity created by exclusion cannot be an Acts 2 Fellowship since Jesus never taught exclusion. Jesus did, however, teach us Co-Leadership long before it was an idea in the complementary minds of Ludeman and Erlandson. Our problem continues to be Authority, scale and the deceptions of the Enemy's hierarchical World OS. After providing us so very many historical examples of the problems with authority, disunity, exclusion, productivity focus, scale and misguided individuated benevolence - his Son came to teach us his Unity OS at the price of his own life. That's how committed Adonai is – Unity At All Costs!

When *personal holiness* is our response to the Creator of the universe drawing us to himself, we are on a solid Foundation. From there all things are possible. If we will but make *him* King of our lives, the Head, the brains of the operation – he will Unite us with our alphas to accomplish more than we could ever dream, hope or imagine.

Chapter Thirteen

Co-Discipleship With Alphas: Discerning The Appropriate Dialogue

Over the last two thousand plus years, the followers of Jesus have been sharing how Jesus warned that a portion of the religious leaders of their day had been borne of a Corrupt lineage and were intent upon using their positions for personal advancement and the Control and Direction of people.

He shared that another portion of the religious leaders of their day were simply well-intentioned Fools, unaware of the harm they were bringing upon themselves and others by their ignorance.

He went on to explain a third portion of the people who he called Wise, their wisdom coming from their understanding of the ways of God. He advised that the wise could be counted upon to become wise and effective leaders in the service of the people.

For all of our benefit, he further explained how we might tell the difference between the Corrupt, the Fool and the Wise: through the behaviors which set them apart. People of these three types are identified in detail throughout Old Testament scripture. In some cases, the Corrupt may be better described as Evil.

Henry Cloud, a Christian psychologist and highly respected corporate consultant has some tips for working with The Wise, The Foolish and The Corrupt/Evil. Each require a different approach:

> The diagnostic question is: What does a person do when the truth comes to them?
>
> THE WISE: When light (truth) comes to them, that person adjusts themselves to match the light. When truth comes, they change something. Proverbs says, "Correct a wise person, and he will be wiser still." David said, "A righteous man will strike me and it will be a blessing." Talk to wise people. Talking helps because someone is listening.
>
> Another quality is that they smile, and thank you when you give them feedback! When asked, "Would you like some feedback?" the Wise will say, "Yeah, give me a gift."

So, what do you do with the Wise? Talk to them, talking helps because someone is listening. Give them feedback, coaching, and keep them challenged to help them keep growing.

THE FOOLISH: We make assumptions as leaders. We think people are actually LISTENING to us. The fool may be the smartest person at the table, but when the light shows up, they adjust the light because it hurts their eyes. What do you do when that person is allergic to the truth? They are where they are because of what they can do, but they try to dim the light and adjust the truth. The fool will try to minimize it, excuse it or shoot the messenger. They deny it's reality, they minimize it and externalize it ("If you would just… it would be OK."), and you don't get a smiley face.

A lot of times they get angry, and have the meeting after the meeting and find somebody to triangulate with, and now you're the problem - and they split the organization. Every time you talk to a person like this, they do not own it. If their first reflective move is external, let that be a warning sign - they're squinting at the light at that point. (Assuming we are right, and they are not... But sometimes we are the Fool in this situation because we are the one who is wrong. We are the one who is squinting. Don't be a Fool!)

Here's what the Bible says, and here's what all research supports: Do not confront or correct a fool, lest you incur insults upon yourself. Stop talking! Talk, rather, about how talking doesn't help. Take the talk above the weeds and talk about the pattern. This is where you can get soft and loving. Maybe they are foolish because of reasons related to shame and insecurity.

People want feedback in different ways. Find a way that works. "I want to know how I can talk to you so that when we talk it makes a difference; and what we will do if I do what you ask, and then nothing happens. I want to plan for the conversation after this conversation if there are poor consequences."

Fools do not change when truth comes to them that they can get rid of. Fools change when truth comes to them that they must camp out in and feel; when the pain of not changing becomes greater than the pain of changing. You know what I love about fools (besides me being a recovering fool)? There is great HOPE for Fools. Jesus died for Fools, all of us are foolish to some degree…… If we will stop assuming that they're listening and instead help them to understand (because there are always consequences and external structure involved), Fools can change and you can redeem a person and a giftedness (and a soul) – if you do what leadership requires. But that takes guts.

THE EVIL: They have destruction in their hearts and they want to inflict pain. It's hard for optimistic people to believe this, but there really are bad people in this world. You can't talk to them and you can't fix them. Paul says to reject a divisive person after the 2nd warning. Have nothing to do with them. We have to go into protection mode with evil people. Lawyers and police are sometimes needed.

What does a person do when the truth comes to them? Since everyone is not the same, you cannot deal with everyone the same. But that's what responsible leaders do, and that's the mistake.

In just a few paragraphs, Henry Cloud provided us dialogue processes for Mutual Accountability and Relational Co-Discipleship with anyone (and them for us if we have Foolishly postured an Authoritarian position).

Pat Lencione, in The Advantage, has devoted an entire book to helping us with how to approach such conversations. When we choose Unity at all costs Co-Leadership and Relational Mutually Accountable Co-Discipleship, we can Dialogue with stubborn know-it-alls, fisherman, business owners, tax collectors and prostitutes – and them with us! Fundamental Attribution Errors between people abound in our churches and among those of us in organizational leadership of all kinds. We can overcome these! The Foundational Operating Error of the World OS, however, cannot be overcome. It must be completely replaced with the Unity OS and Structure for The Body.

If we will do the hard work of leadership, it starts by looking first at our assumptions for organizational operating system and structure, then for disunity and finally for missing parts. Knowledge is not typically the weakest link in the chain, and it comes easily enough in the forms of the many reference materials and experts available. The greatest issue in any organization is an Authoritarian Operating System and Structure because it will breed mistrust and result in Relational Blocks being thrown up as protection. These create the leader blind spots that keep us from understanding our obstacles and accomplishing our goals. Iron that sharpens iron in True Unity reveals our collective blind spots and facilitates our collective discernment of the mind of Christ the Head – and, in it, his grace is sufficient for us.

Another Approach for The Evil

Most of the aforementioned advice by Henry Cloud is in discussion of *relationships in our entities*. What about our service to others personally as individuals? In his book *The Jesus I Never Knew,* (while linking the absolutes of the Beatitudes and Jesus' actions on the cross) Philip Yancey reminds us that Adonai would additionally have us consider how we might otherwise engage with The Evil. He quotes M. Scott Peck first:

> I cannot be any more specific about the methodology of love than to quote these words of an old priest who spent many years in the battle: "There are dozens of ways to deal with evil and several ways to conquer it. All of them are facets of the truth that the only ultimate way to conquer evil is to let it be smothered within a willing, living human being. When it is absorbed there like blood in a sponge or a spear into one's heart, it loses its power and goes no further."
>
> The healing of evil – scientifically or otherwise – can be accomplished only by the love of individuals. A willing sacrifice is required . . . I do not know how this occurs. But I know that it does . . . Whenever this happens there is a slight shift in the balance of power in the world.

You might pause here to reflect on that, asking the Father who dwells within you to do his works…

Yancey goes on to say:

> What changed history was that . . . God himself had chosen the way of weakness. The cross redefines God as One who was willing to relinquish power for the sake of love. Jesus became, in Dorothy Solle's phrase, "God's unilateral disarmament."
>
> Power, no matter how well intentioned, tends to cause suffering. Love, being vulnerable, absorbs it. In a point of convergence on a hill called Calvary, God renounced the one for the sake of the other.

If you have taken *any* Authority, you hold a measure of power. If you use that power to accomplish your desires, your goals, your will - with your will-power - people will suffer. Adonai would have us abandon the power of Authority so as to operate in Unity, in agreement, *iron sharpening iron*, without rubber stamps, without subtle Leverage or Coercion. In harmony. His kingdom coming, his will being done on earth as it is in heaven.

The foundation of his will for us rests upon synergizing One-ness with him, him in us and us in him - becoming perfectly One.

****

Be Willing To Make A Difference: Co-Discipleship

I just had another far too common conversation. A church staff member has resigned after witnessing their Senior Pastor go eyeball-to-eyeball (yet again) with a staff member who disagreed with him. There was only one raised voice in the room, that of the pastor. His message was that he didn't have time for debate, that there is too much to do, that they can't sit around and argue about it, and since he is the one in charge – it's his way or the highway. Leader Replication is in full swing.

Others of us accomplish the same thing with a look, a stare, a cold shoulder, a critical comment, inapplicable scripture, a well phrased sentence of subtle Leverage or Coercion . . . the list goes on.

This pastor has a history of using subtle and not-so-subtle Coercive Leverage, and the remaining faithful are seemingly under his thumb – numb. Whatever productivity he thinks he is making is just more Deception from the Enemy. Alpha Reconcilers will eventually rise up and oust him. (Updating this since the time of my original writing, they have.)

"When we started as a church plant, it was a shared adventure." The HR Director of a 20,000 person church continued on to say, "It all takes a nosedive when any leader begins to think that future success rides upon their shoulders."

Where Co-Leadership is not, Co-Discipleship cannot be. If Co-Discipleship is limited, so too will be individual wholeness and True Unity (though faux unity may be observed). Where there is a small amount of Co-Leadership, there will be a small amount of Co-Discipleship. The measure with which you give shall be given back to you. Empty yourself of power in Mutual

Accountability, and you (plural) will become Powerful (by the power of the Holy Spirit). If you consider yourself a leader, follow the Direction of Adonai, your Spiritual Leader. Reconcile your position to his collectively, discern the Mind of Christ, and therefore that of the Father. Follow Christ collectively and you (plural) will receive Power from on high that only Love may bring.

Our Adversary's Deception adds pressure, creates singularity, steals our time, creates counter-testimony for Enemy use and limits our productivity - as measured in changed lives.

Proverbs 14:12
There is a way that seems right to a man, but its end is the way to death.

Here are some Director statements of disharmony or faux one-ness, that may serve as red flags. If we will effectively Co-Lead, these should cause us to pause for engagement in Mutually Accountable Co-Discipleship:

- We're not ready for that yet.....
- Thank you, but we can't afford staff for that yet.....
- He/she is so busy right now, we just can't add that on, too.
- That's his area, talk to him about it, I can't.
- Trust me, ... Trust me, ...
- I'll do it, but you have to promise to back off and give me space...
- I'll take it from here...
- You guys have got to stop micromanaging me........
- I know what we said, but I had to make a decision in the moment.....
- You guys don't know this stuff like I do, just let me handle it.....
- It won't work if somebody else does it....
- I'll do it, but I don't want any help cuz they'll just slow me down....
- It's *my* vision, so *I* have to lead it *my* way...

We can easily respond to such statements by pointing to our values. If these values are not clear throughout the organization, you may be sure that the above types of statements are being made by Individuated Leaders and that *Satan is crouching at the door*.

Genesis 4:7
If you do well, will you not be accepted? And if you do not do well, sin is crouching at the door. Its desire is contrary to you, but you must rule over it."

We are committed to:

- One-ness: Him in us and us in Him
- Acts of Love & Intercession
- Hearts after the Father in attitudes consistent with the Beatitudes: Jesus' attitudes
- Fruit of the Spirit Language & Actions
- Connecting & Inviting
- Relational Mutually Accountable Co-Discipleship
- Development of Balanced Director/Reconciler Teams in Co-Leadership
- Leadership Teams that Do Not Have or Use Hierarchy/Authority
- Unity/Unanimity in Decisions & Actions
- Groups of Teams and Teams of Groups
- Leadership Development at All Levels
- Advisory Forums at ALL levels
    - *Collective* discernment of the Input of ALL People
    - Has God brought us a Leader Out Of Nowhere, now here?
- Facilitating Spirit-Led Self-Selection of Service

****

Be Willing To Make A Difference: Mentoring

As a child I remember listening to my father and his friends talking about their eventual retirement. One said they would spend it hunting, another said fishing, another hitting the casino, another woodworking in their shop at home and one said doing landscaping and gardening around their home.

Other than the casino, it was great to hear that they had been doing these things with their children as they raised them. But with a slight modification, they could still be doing them as mentors during retirement with people of need in their communities.

These days many are finding great joy in doing these hobbies with troubled teens, rehabilitating felons and alongside lonely seniors. Jesus invited the apostles to become fishers of men. How about hunters of men, people taking a chance on men and woodworkers training up young men? The same could be said for bankers and lawyers and accountants. What a waste it is when the collective wisdom of the elders in our communities not only retire from their careers, but from engagement with those they could most easily support in their love of the Lord while doing activities that share their knowledge and skills! There is no more joyful and rewarding life than one of connecting with others in life-on-life opportunities.

Still others are working with our more promising youth to share and show what it looks like to be in relationship with the living God. Led by him, avoiding the pitfalls of life. Avoiding isolation, sadness and perhaps incarceration.

****

We are the ones now, who must decide what we will do with the information that Jesus has taught while the Father has been in us is doing his works, and whether or not we will follow the leading of the Holy Spirit in alpha development and mentorship. Will we recognize that the need is so great that we simply must be willing to *become* transparent relationally for the development of more unpaid Co-Leading alphas? Church and government leaders, will you please facilitate that? Ephesians 4 tells us that *"The role of the leader is to equip/prepare/facilitate the people to acts of service."* Accomplish your will in us, O God!

Father, forgive us our sin. We, the people of your church in the United States, have not taken care of our neighbors, widows and orphans. We have not been without impact, but we have left such a large vacuum of need! We offer our gifts at your altar and send our taxes in to our governments, but we do not sufficiently engage, and relationally attend, to the vast need.

Many of us go to our churches to learn each week and gather with our friends to talk about the deteriorating state of the world, but we do not personally engage to change it either. We are like the perennial college student who never graduates, gets a job, and puts the learnings to work. While many of us look forward to retirement and the opportunity to spend great amounts of time on our hobbies, people of need whom we could otherwise greatly help are going unserved. You have every right to let our complaints to you fall on deaf ears. Unite your people to more productive service, O God!

How did we come to the place where we expect our government to take care of our impoverished neighbors? While we have been so blessed by you, so many were raised by parents who do not know you, or did not sufficiently share your great desire to love and lead us to abundant lives of Joy. They could have been us!

Though we have been blessed to be a blessing, we justify our inactivity by pointing to the role of government and the risk of our personal safety, though Jesus, you went to the impoverished with a tender caring heart. Yours is the way, the truth and the life! Build us up for the bringing of your kingdom into the hearts, souls and minds of people everywhere – that none should perish. Lord of the harvest, send laborers!

Chapter Fourteen

Scaling Up With Our Alphas: Components And Processes That Must Remain As We Scale

Unity

Unity is almost automatic in our church plants, but we often fail in relationships as we scale in size. If we allow Authority to influence our behavior *outside* of our church relationships, we will certainly transition back to it *in* our church relationships – especially as we scale. Remember, any blending of the World OS and his is an improvement upon it and an adulteration of his. If we are to sustainably scale with him from me to us, to church plant, to large church, and for the transformation of our communities and nation – he would have us use purely his. If we want to change the world, it starts and stays with growing the "us".

Give all of us this day our daily bread. Forgive us when we cross the line as we forgive all of those who cross the line against us. Lead us that we not enter into temptation. Deliver us from evil.

Balance: Triune Maturity

Made in Adonai's Triune image we tend to prefer to operate in one more than the other two. That is a gifting, but then we also have a tendency to over-use that gifting. The old saying is that to a carpenter, every problem looks like it needs a saw and hammer. To every Director, every problem looks like it needs their insightful strategic direction. To every Reconciler, every problem looks like it needs better cooperation for greater synergy. To every Active Implementer, every problem looks like it needs more people in support of leadership.

As an individual, which role do you tend to function in most often? As a triune individual, do you know when to tell the Director in you to take a seat and listen to the Reconciler or Active Implementer *in you*? Do you know when to tell the Director in you to take a seat and listen to the Reconciler or Active Implementer *in someone else*? Which triune portion are *you* most gifted to *lead* with? Which do you most prefer?

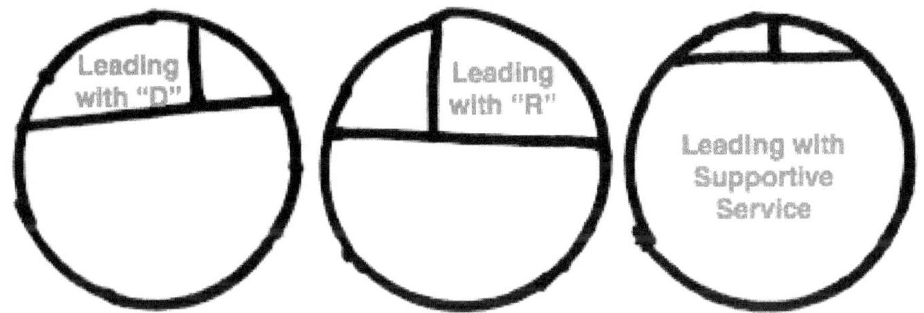

Are you allowing the Holy Spirit to strengthen your other two muscles? Are you becoming more and more balanced and capable (mature) in the use of each of the three? Is your organization?

If you prefer Supportive Service and a Director leader has just said or done something that was highly productive, but damaging to relationship – are you strong enough to let your Reconciler speak up? (Whether or not the other person is likely to listen?) Are you afraid to do so because it may not be well received, or could mean the loss of your job? Can you say it well relationally so that *iron sharpens iron respectfully and with a desire for oneness*? Can those in your organization? (I again refer you to The Advantage for sample conversations.) Collectively, do you additionally have Unity Values that may be pointed to for reference?

Remembering our Self-Selection conversation with Tom, if Mutually Accountable Co-Discipleship is expected throughout your organization, you may speak up safely because no one has the Authority to fire. If we are all committed to having the attitudes of the Beatitudes spoken in fruit of the Spirit language and in Relational Mutually Accountable Co-Discipleship, the extent of our risk is whether or not we follow through with it to grow in balance, and so mature together in one-ness doing so - otherwise, we will have begun to Self-Select our way out.

If you prefer Supportive Service and a Reconciler leader has ground to a halt, even though in the meeting all agreed to take the strategic action – are you strong enough to let your Director speak up? Can you say it well relationally so that *iron sharpens iron*? Can those in your organization?

We are all parts of one Body, none better than another. All are deserving of being heard. We must always keep in mind that we never really know when the Holy Spirit will be showing up with a word of Encouragement or Correction. Do we have eyes that see and ears that hear? Does our organization? Fruit of the Spirit language and actions produce Unity and sustainable productivity led *by* the power of the Holy Spirit - our Helper, Advisor and Wonderful Counselor. Otherwise:

Matthew 13:14-15

14 Indeed, in their case the prophecy of Isaiah is fulfilled that says: "''You will indeed hear but never understand, and you will indeed see but never perceive." 15 For this people's heart has grown dull, and with their ears they can barely hear, and their eyes they have closed, lest they should see with their eyes and hear with their ears and understand with their heart and turn, and I would heal them.'

Advisory Forums

These occurred quite informally and maybe even unknowingly when we were a church plant. Because we were quite small in size, we often did them alone after service or with 2-3 over lunch. These were important meetings in which the people we eventually came to know and trust offered suggestions and support for an idea whose time had come. As we will describe shortly, we tend to miss these opportunities as we scale.

God's advice sometimes comes to us from the Holy Spirit directly to our spirit and sometimes from another person led by the Spirit to our spirit. Either way, it is Advisory. This Advice may come to us in many forms but because Love does not demand his own way, he gives us the right to accept it (accept him) or reject it (reject him). We must take care to avoid syllogism & FAEs and instead utilize appropriate Advisory discernment processes with a broad complement of giftedness present. You'll need your opposites present to discern clearly.

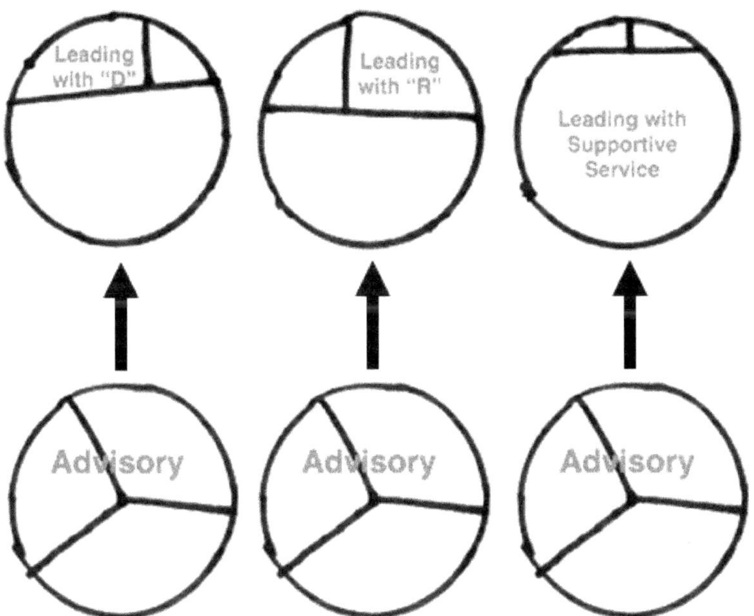

What environment are you in? What is the situation? Are you being Advised? Might he be speaking through you with his Advice? Maybe both of you are being Advised?

What has God given you to contribute? Does what is occurring call for you to lead with "D" or "R" or Supportive Service? We are to discern.

What is the Spirit Advising? How does he want to make *your* unique Gifts Package useful in this moment? None are like you, not even one. Discern carefully - balance courage with patience - lest you miss his purpose for the moment.

"D"s, is this an "R" or Supportive Service moment for you? Be careful of your tendency.

"R"s, is this a "D" or Supportive Service moment for you? Be careful of your tendency.

"Supportive Servers in Active Implementation", is this an "R" or a "D" moment for you? Be careful of your tendency.

Organizations, is your balance trending toward out-of-balance with "D" or "R" right now? Are you listening to the Advice of your opposites? With ears that hear?

Continue Connecting the *Whole* Body

As you look around, what is needed? How might you be useful as a ligament that could Connect a Body Part that is missing? Not only is the Spirit

Advising us of our role in the moment, but if there is to be productivity, we need to be looking for missing Body Parts. God does not Direct work without also providing resources – are we looking with eyes that see and ears that hear?

Prepare for Evolution to Scale

Church plants typically consider Advice informally and with great Unity in the beginning, but then typically lose it as they achieve scale. When young, they feel compelled to listen to Advisors and seek out the Connections God is providing as they serve to grow his church. As Advisors came up to speak with them after service, they had plenty of time and a great desire to have ears that hear - so that they might have eyes to see who God was bringing them and for what purpose - even those that looked like stubborn know-it-alls, fisherman, business owners, tax collectors and prostitutes! We typically feel less compelled to engage them as we achieve scale because success brings the funds that reduce the sense of need that we formerly had – and permit us to rationalize in FAEs.

As we scale up and prioritize maintaining Unity as God maintains Unity, we move as One as God moves as One. We remain in discernment mode at all times to spot deviations from Unity as they present themselves and to pause for restoration. These are the Mutual Accountability and Co-Discipleship opportunities that bear much fruit. As we scale, we must recognize our tendency toward Control (that would have us dis-Connect) and instead continue to engage in the difficult dialogue where *iron sharpens iron*, a brother or sister is won and God is glorified by the productive synergies provided. The alternative is Dismissive. May we see these as opportunities to embrace, not agony to avoid – and so engage in the hard work of Relational Mutually Accountable Co-Discipleship.

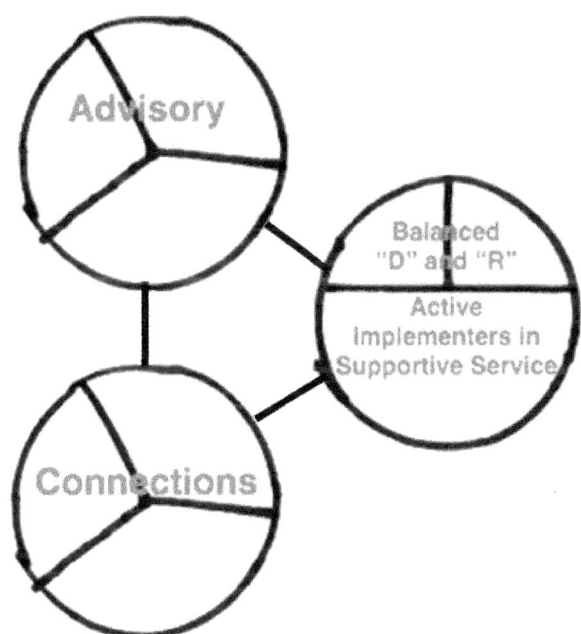

Continue the Co-Led Co-Discipled Process in Mutual Accountability as you Scale

Whether you are approached with Advice for an idea by an alpha or you are the one approaching an alpha to Advise that you would like them to consider involvement in something, the process is much the same. We start off by saying yes. Yes, we agree that something needs to be done. Yes, we agree that what is being described is one way to approach it. Yes, we agree that God will illuminate the best way for us if we will work together to solve it. Yes, we agree that others will be needed to lend a hand to accomplish it. Yes, we agree that a group of people should be put into the same room to brainstorm taking the vision to reality. Yes, we agree that you (the alpha) could make a great contribution given your passion and the need for leadership giftedness.

From here, we can take the conversation to the next level. This is the point at which Co-Leadership, with an expectation for Relational Mutual Accountability in Co-Discipleship, is described as the best way toward accomplishment.

"This is a huge need. I'm very excited by the prospects of actually pulling it off. Would you mind if we took a little time together to talk about how we do

leadership here and how you could be a part of that? You've probably heard us describe this previously regarding another effort, but just to be sure, I'd like to lay out our Co-Leadership process for the initiation of new ministry or the expansion of what exists. We do this whenever a new idea comes forward."

"From time to time we have these things we call Advisory Forums. They occur at every level of ministry – top to bottom. When an idea comes forward, we determine the urgency and setup a time for the idea to be presented in the most appropriate Forum. Whenever possible, we wait for a few of these to accumulate before setting a meeting – but if the need seems urgent we put one together ASAP. Our Advisory Forums are designed to include all of the broad giftedness that we have in our associated leadership positions so that an idea is not inadvertently blocked by a person who doesn't really understand what is being shared. We are trying to avoid anything that would work like a "gatekeeper" and instead give us the best chance of understanding it by virtue of the broad giftedness in the room. Is that OK?"

"Our goal is to figure out a way to say, "Yes.". So, if we assume right now that this idea (or some form of it) will be put to use, we also want to be sure that you understand how we will want it led. Other than your reputation, we really don't know you that well. But even for those we know quite well we still use this same process. Basically, we ask you to co-lead with at least one other person that we will either approve or, if we are all in agreement, provide you. I can explain it better over coffee or lunch, but all we are trying to do is put together a balanced passionate leadership team from the outset. We think God has been clear about this being the best way, so if that's OK with you, can a few of us get together to talk it through? If so, we'll put this forward right after that and we can bring it to an Advisory Forum together."

The Core Elements

Unity, Balance, Advisory Forums, Connections, Preparing for Evolution to Scale, and Continuing in Co-Leadership & Mutually Accountable Co-Discipleship are described over a meal or coffee, including the expectation that the new team will form a small group and meet together to be known by each other, operate in transparency and bring support to each other's lives.

(If this is to expand an existing team they would join that group in some way.)

"Here's a copy of our values, but I'm sure you've seen them on the wall there. It's important to recognize that our values are first for Unity and that we move as One or we don't move at all. The team that is formed will need to be diverse to be sure that every decision is thought through from every perspective before implementation. We hope to develop a balance of passionate Directors and Reconcilers with disparate personalities that draw many more into Supportive Service. Expertise and/or passionate interest in this area is a given. If a decision cannot be made unanimously, you must know that we expect that decision to be delayed while the minority view or views are fully considered. We frequently find that these views are very helpful in keeping implementation and integration relational, and that brings greater synergy which eventually becomes more highly productive. Otherwise, our tendencies toward productivity sometimes cause us to try to build on the fly - unintentionally causing relational damage that leads some to dis-Connect. Relational processes might take more time, but they're much more productive in the long run."

So where is the risk? We are not letting loose an untried potentially immature D or R alpha leader. What we are doing instead is temporarily placing tried and true alpha Ds and Rs with him/her for the productive purpose of learning Co-Leadership and the relational process of Mutual Accountability in Co-Discipleship. Doing so, we may expect God to develop talmidim as Jesus teaches, the Spirit leads and the Father within us does his works.

Given the typically Director-led World OS Culture that surrounds us, the real concern is whether or not we have enough mature alpha Reconcilers to go around. Needs are great! If we do not have development processes occurring to prepare our alphas, we will not be prepared for their optimal release into co-leadership. As you will see as we proceed, Jehovah Jireh has probably already provided you more high-capacity leaders than you now have in paid staff. His desire is to turbo-charge your collective efforts by the power of the Holy Spirit, increasing productivity beyond that which you could otherwise ever dream, hope or imagine possible.

Chapter Fifteen

More Paid Staff Or More Unpaid Co-Leaders?

James 1:27
Religion that is pure and undefiled before God, the Father, is this: to visit orphans and widows in their affliction, and to keep oneself unstained from the world.

The best boss of all time, God has given us all of the high-capacity Director and Reconciler leaders that we need, and he has given you yours because they need you! We cannot rationalize away the reality that we are to find ways to serve together with our unpaid alphas. Once we set aside our Authority mind set and instead describe a co-led/co-discipled path in One-ness – we find ourselves in a very workable environment - like we had as a church plant.

Church plants need everyone. There are never enough people serving like Paul the tentmaker and rarely enough money available to make multiple staff hires. In a growing church plant the norm is ministries filled with non-paid people serving. Relationships between the founders and these new arrivals easily blossom into solid relationships (due to the nearly automatic Mutually Accountable Co-Discipleship that occurs in the close proximity of church plant relationships) and a variety of non-paid ministry Co-Leaders.

Quality talmidim relationships changed the world after Jesus. Our Acts 2 Fellowships brought great Joy and changed the world around us as church plants. Just as Jesus prepared his talmidim in advance for the releasing of them after his resurrection, we must be preparing our alphas for what Adonai will be leading us into next. Quality alpha talmidim are the answer to what will otherwise become our at-scale problems.

This is the national average for congregational involvement according to a study by Leadership Network. Amazingly, it is quite consistent regardless of congregational size:

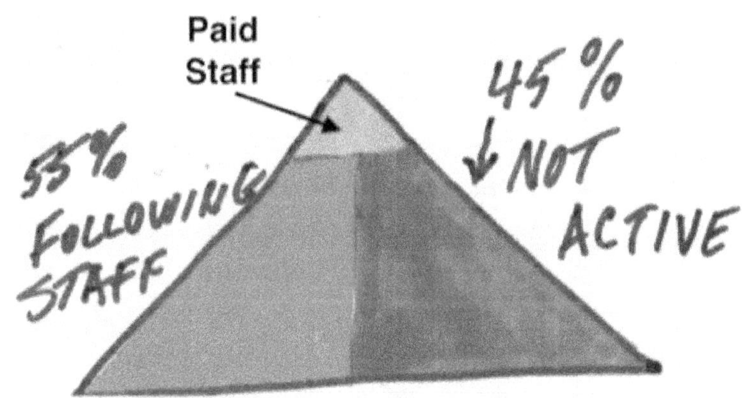

All too frequently, new ministry will not be initiated unless there is sufficient funding to staff a position to oversee it. The hierarchical World OS requires money for the hiring of people to get things done. The Unity OS is full of people called to lead and serve for free while they earn income elsewhere. Many of our inactive Supportive Servers do not serve because our World OS preferences cannot afford to hire and Leverage the leaders needed to oversee them!

Many an alpha has approached an Individuated Leader about new areas of service only to be told "We can't afford that yet." Funding of oversight, not the availability of Active Implementers ready for Supportive Service, determines Kingdom expansion.

Director alphas say, "You can't Control volunteers. We cannot expand ministry if God isn't providing the funds for staff oversight." As they leave out those who are passionately gifted to lead and serve in areas not staffed, they miss out on ministry that would lead more *inactives* into passionately aligned service on teams of diverse giftedness – for the benefit of *the widows and the orphans*. Clearly, these Directors require the ability to Leverage people to Control productivity at a level that they think they can *Man*age.

Under our breath, and in staff meetings, others add that our attempts at involving non-paid leaders always seem to fail due to their spiritual immaturity. But the Deception of our Adversary leads us to assumptions that are simply not true. We cite examples of their failings, but do not recognize that *we* are actually the ones who failed *them* due to our bias for Hierarchy and Individuated Authority. I've seen it time and time again!

In my experience, the best of leaders do not need to Leverage, *Man*age, *Man*ipulate or *Man*euver. These leaders are so adept at drawing out all of the information from their paid and unpaid team members that it is a Uniting process whereby every person is *fully bought in* to what they were a part of deciding. Mutually Accountable, this is Co-Leadership and Co-Discipleship accomplished through conversations that Pat Lencione clearly describes in The Advantage.

The only productivity Adonai really cares about is the developing of life saving relationships. When our number one priority is relationship building, he will make us useful to develop more and more talmidim who will develop more and more talmidim, who will develop more and more talmidim. The development of people and relationships broadens the *quality* and *trustworthiness* of our paid and unpaid leadership *base*. It is what succeeded most when we were a church plant, and must continue as we scale.

Some say that building relationships with each *at scale* is impossible – *but that is because they never had a view for it and so did not prepare for it.* As we scale, the number of people who we must come to know, grow and develop is not nearly as insurmountable as we may think:

Typically:

- *6%-10% of the population are high-capacity leaders*
- *45% of the people in any given church are inactive*

Therefore,

- *3%-5% of The Body are inactive high-capacity alphas*
- *If weekly attendance is 100, you have 3-5 latent high-capacity alphas to identify, Relationally Co-Disciple and facilitate to active service to lead Supportive Servers in Active Implementation. With 1,000 in weekly attendance, that number would be 30-50.*

Development of the people associated with the above percentages is entirely reasonable!

We need to be identifying the remaining 3%-5% of inactive alphas for Leadership Development. Many successfully provide such targeted Co-Discipleship for their tent-making high-capacity alphas through Co-Discipleship Training groups of 10-20 people. If leadership will avail themselves in the Small Group environment to get know each alpha individually, by the end of the year everyone will know what everyone else is passionate about leading, have worked a process with them to identify their Co-Leader(s) and have begun inviting Active Implementers to join them through one of the many facilitative Connections Team processes.

Accomplishing it requires that we re-learn Co-Leadership alongside high-capacity non-paid leaders as we did originally in our church plants. Unless there is a Co-Discipleship/Co-Leadership development process worthy of high-capacity *leaders of leaders* who would serve in a non-paid way – we cannot. We also need to implement Co-Discipleship/Co-Leadership development tracks for the high-capacity leaders in our congregations who are new believers. The *Life* section is one tried and true way of doing so.

Though it may seem slow initially, it is faster and far more effective in the long run as leader multiplication begets leader multiplication that begets leader multiplication - *such that we are ready for life-on-life success at scale.*

Nothing will happen unless we agree together that it should happen. If we wish to follow Jesus' Lead we will accept our strong-willed alpha "Peters", and Advise them of our need for them in service. If our "Peter" begins to wander off toward individuated leadership, our alpha Reconciler will know how to respond to that. As maturity grows through relationship with our co-leading Reconciler, broader leadership capacity is gained, more Active Implementers in Supportive Service are drained away from the 45% inactive and there is more left to share with the widows and the orphans.

We all know that we have to prioritize life-on-life relationships no matter our scale, but we will never succeed without unpaid alphas! If we are unwilling to do the hard work of leadership, *we* are the biggest obstacles to engaging the currently inactive!

Though it may seem slower initially, it is faster and far more effective in the long run as leader multiplication begets leader multiplication that begets leader multiplication - such that we are ready for life-on-life success at scale!

Search Out and Engage Your Alphas

As we frequently identify, high-capacity leaders go unused both in their area of expertise and their demonstrably broad leadership capacity. Exaggerating the point, with a Steve Jobs in our congregation, no one would expect him to serve under our Technology leader, but it is quite analogous to what we actually do because our Military Chain of Command Organizational Structure holds that staff position accountable.

Typically, neither do we invite him into a high-capacity leadership role where both could be used. We avoid strong-willed intellect, do not get to know them, do not trust those we do not know and have no *purpose-filled* processes in place for them to be able to get to know *us* personally – warts and all.

Some will describe already having opportunities to get to know people through *proving ground* ministries like greeting, ushering and such, but this is a waste of alpha giftedness. Others would describe new member processes or 101, 201, 301 classes where the truly interested may meet us, us them and see where it goes from there. While these are well and good, they may also be the legalistic obstacles we place so as to filter out the mavericks who are unlikely to attend. Justifying the shrug of our shoulders, we say, "See? Where are they?"

In my experience, these proving ground processes draw Active Implementers for Supportive Service, but not alpha leaders. Then, due to the insufficient number of alpha leaders needed to lead them well, these Active Implementers once again fall away and return to inactivity.

Explain and implement Co-Discipleship/Co-Leadership development tracks for your high-capacity alphas. Seek them out. Offer full transparency. Do the hard work of Relational Co-Discipleship and let the Spirit work. Why do they need to prove themselves in some way first? Jesus didn't do that with Peter, and he didn't require it of us! They are in our midst. God has given them to *us* to support in their *becoming*. He is allowing us to *participate* with him in the development of his talmidim – that none should perish. That our Joy may be complete.

We say we strive for excellence in all we do, so let's invite, accept and integrate people like a Steve Jobs in Co-Leadership and learn how to lead *with* them. Our Authoritarian assumptions lead us to conflicts that purpose-filled Co-Leadership with the expectation of Relational Mutually Accountable Co-Discipleship would not. Co-Discipleship with alphas is more difficult due to their great intellect, the requirement for *our* transparency - and the *pride* many of us have that does not want them to know us that well. *Posturing* on the responsibilities under our "Authority" blocks their involvement and our acceptance of their Advice – and the 45% remain inactive while *widows and orphans* struggle all around us.

We are committed to:

- One-ness: Him in us and us in Him
- Acts of Love & Intercession
- Hearts after the Father in attitudes consistent with the Beatitudes: Jesus' attitudes
- Fruit of the Spirit Language & Actions
- Connecting & Inviting
- Relational Mutually Accountable Co-Discipleship
- Development of Balanced Director/Reconciler Teams in Co-Leadership
- Leadership Teams that Do Not Have or Use Hierarchy/Authority
- Unity/Unanimity in Decisions & Actions
- Groups of Teams and Teams of Groups
- Leadership Development at All Levels
- Advisory Forums at ALL levels
    - *Collective* discernment of the Input of ALL People
    - Has God brought us a Leader Out Of Nowhere, now here?
- Facilitating Spirit-Led Self-Selection of Service

It is critical that we see every person as a Connection through which God may offer us his Advice and lead us to the Connection of yet another Body Part. Connecting *by every supporting ligament*, we need all of our alphas if we will activate the inactive. If we will scale as God scales himself for us, we need to lock arms and move as one as Adonai moves as One. We exist in the safety of his unendingly patient and caring relational way - allowing us to accept him or reject him. May we be willing to do the same with our more difficult alphas!

****

Multiple scripture references indicate the need for us to support paid leaders. Still, Paul adds perspective in consideration of our alphas and in avoidance of payment:

1 Corinthians 9:3-23

3 This is my defense to those who would examine me. 4 Do we not have the right to eat and drink? 5 Do we not have the right to take along a believing wife, as do the other apostles and the brothers of the Lord and Cephas? 6 Or is it only Barnabas and I who have no right to refrain from working for a living? 7 Who serves as a soldier at his own expense? Who plants a vineyard without eating any of its fruit? Or who tends a flock without getting some of the milk?

8 Do I say these things on human authority? Does not the Law say the same? 9 For it is written in the Law of Moses, "You shall not muzzle an ox when it treads out the grain." Is it for oxen that God is concerned? 10 Does he not certainly speak for our sake? It was written for our sake, because the plowman should plow in hope and the thresher thresh in hope of sharing in the crop. 11 If we have sown spiritual things among you, is it too much if we reap material things from you? 12 If others share this rightful claim on you, do not we even more?

Nevertheless, we have not made use of this right, but we endure anything rather than put an obstacle in the way of the gospel of Christ. 13 Do you not know that those who are employed in the temple service get their food from the temple, and those who serve at the altar share in the sacrificial offerings? 14 In the same way, the Lord commanded that those who proclaim the gospel should get their living by the gospel.

15 But I have made no use of any of these rights, nor am I writing these things to secure any such provision. For I would rather die than have anyone deprive me of my ground for boasting. 16 For if I preach the gospel, that gives me no ground for boasting. For necessity is laid upon me. Woe to me if I do not preach the gospel! 17 For if I do this of my own will, I have a reward, but if not of my own will, I am still entrusted with a stewardship. 18 What then is my reward? That in my preaching I may present the gospel free of charge, so as not to make full use of my right in the gospel.

19 For though I am free from all, I have made myself a servant to all, that I might win more of them. 20 To the Jews I became as a Jew, in order to win Jews. To those under the law I became as one under the law (though not being myself under the law) that I might win those under the law. 21 To those outside the law I became as one outside the law (not being outside the law of God but under the law of Christ) that I might win those outside the law. 22 To the weak I became weak, that I might win the weak. I have become all things to all people, that by all means I might save some. 23 I do it all for the sake of the gospel, that I may share with them in its blessings.

1 Thessalonians 4:9-12

9 Now concerning brotherly love you have no need for anyone to write to you, for you yourselves have been taught by God to love one another, 10 for that indeed is what you are doing to all the brothers throughout Macedonia. But we urge you, brothers, to do this more and more, 11 and to aspire to live quietly, and to mind your own affairs, and to work with your hands, as we instructed you, 12 so that you may walk properly before outsiders and be dependent on no one.

2 Thessalonians 3:6-15

6 Now we command you, brothers, in the name of our Lord Jesus Christ, that you keep away from any brother who is walking in idleness and not in accord with the tradition that you received from us. 7 For you yourselves know how you ought to imitate us, because we were not idle when we were with you, 8 nor did we eat anyone's bread without paying for it, but with toil and labor we worked night and day, that we might not be a burden to any of you. 9 It was not because we do not have that right, but to give you in ourselves an example to imitate. 10 For even when we were with you, we would give you this command: If anyone is not willing to work, let him not eat. 11 For we hear that some among you walk in idleness, not busy at work, but busybodies. 12 Now such persons we command and encourage in the Lord Jesus Christ to do their work quietly and to earn their own living. 13 As for you, brothers, do not grow weary in doing good. 14 If anyone does not obey what we say in this letter, take note of that person, and have nothing to do with him, that he may be ashamed. 15 Do not regard him as an enemy, but warn him as a brother.

Did He Intend It for the Widows and Orphans Instead of Staff?

When Individuated Directors see what needs to be done they hire people to do it – as long as there are funds. If he is the best leader that will ever be, did the Father give you a vision for needed mission but not funding for staff? Are you to step out in faith and hire them anyway? Perhaps it was not about funding or faith, but rather use of nonpaid alphas that you have not taken the time to get to know - *leaving less for the widows and the orphans.*

Maybe he is also trying to protect the person you would have hired away from their current job and the contribution they currently provide for ministry. What if you remember the small church plant days and take time for the unpaid alpha Advisors he has sent you, as you did then?

Why should we expect God to provide us funding if the leader he wants us to Connect with for development already sits among us? Sometimes the "faith" we are leaping with is just us wrestling to maintain or regain Control. And if he lets us do what we want anyway, will he not have a lesson for us to learn about doing it our way farther down the road? Science helps us here also:

- *MOTIVATION: Something that energizes, directs, and sustains behaviors.*
- *INTRINSIC MOTIVATION: Internal desire to perform or accomplish because it provides pleasure.*
- *EXTRINSIC MOTIVATION: Factors external to the individual such as money.*

THE OVERJUSTIFICATION EFFECT: occurs when an external incentive decreases a person's intrinsic motivation to perform a behavior or participate in an activity. Researchers have found that when extrinsic rewards (such as money and prizes) are given for actions that people already find intrinsically rewarding, they will become less internally motivated to pursue those activities in the future.

As we struggle with the leadership demands of growth, the Directors among us will tend to want to hire staff because "You can't Control volunteer leaders." How often it is that those we pull from their careers end up quitting on us. Could it be that we are the cause because we diminished their Intrinsic Motivation and stole their freedom as we transitioned to trying to Control them?

Typically, both Directors and Reconcilers look for a Lever to Control those they think they need. Money and Authority are the very levers many leaders *need* to be "successful". But as Jesus said, it is not to be so among us. Hiring people so as to be able to Control them via Authority is not leadership; it is quite simply our dark side rationalizing - and with every additional staff hired - *leaves less for the widows and the orphans.*

Malachi 3:6-10

6 "For I the Lord do not change; therefore you, O children of Jacob, are not consumed. 7 From the days of your fathers you have turned aside from my statutes and have not kept them. Return to me, and I will return to you, says the Lord of hosts. <u>But you say, 'How shall we return?' 8 Will man rob God? Yet you are robbing me. But you say, 'How have we robbed you?' In your tithes and contributions. 9 You are cursed with a curse, for you are robbing me, the whole nation of you. 10 Bring the full tithe into the storehouse, that there may be food in my house. And thereby put me to the test, says the Lord of hosts, if I will not open the windows of heaven for you and pour down for you a blessing until there is no more need.</u>

Take care! Do not take on the stain of excess staff in the World OS and so rob God of the funds he meant for the widows and orphans. Dear church, test him on this and see if he does not open the windows of heaven and pour down a great blessing!

James 1:26-27

26 If anyone thinks he is religious and does not bridle his tongue but deceives his heart, this person's religion is worthless. 27 Religion that is pure and undefiled before God the Father is this: to visit orphans and widows in their affliction, and to keep oneself unstained from the world.

2 Corinthians 11:7-11

7 Or did I commit a sin in humbling myself so that you might be exalted, because I preached God's gospel to you free of charge? 8 I robbed other churches by accepting support from them in order to serve you. 9 And when I was with you and was in need, I did not burden anyone, for the brothers who came from Macedonia supplied my need. So I refrained and will refrain from burdening you in any way. 10 As the truth of Christ is in me, this boasting of mine will not be silenced in the regions of Achaia. 11 And why? Because I do not love you? God knows I do!

There are many scripture references that prove God's will includes paid staff. But at what point do we cross the line? May we hear the voice of our

Wonderful Counselor Directing us on how to Reconcile the matter before we take the contributions of another tent maker out of play – increasing staff expense and diminishing that which is available for the widows and orphans! He knows the plans he has for us:

1 Samuel 8:6
11 I will rebuke the devourer for you, so that it will not destroy the fruits of your soil, and your vine in the field shall not fail to bear, says the Lord of hosts. 12 Then all nations will call you blessed, for you will be a land of delight, says the Lord of hosts.

Our tendency is to justify the hiring of staff by citing the failures of previous volunteers. While I defend you in your experience, you must admit that the failure was inevitable due to the operating system you were using. The Authoritarian World OS fails us fundamentally as we scale because we cease transparency and so stop meeting with and coming to *know* the new arrivals. Then, somewhat weary, some of our stalwart volunteers quit *us* as well as they tire of the imbalance. We start them off with small tests of their willingness to follow and little by little feed them into the meat-grinder-of-ministry where all of their free time is eventually consumed by our direction. (*You have been faithful over a little; I will set you over much.)*

As they leave us, it reinforces our belief that we must *Man*age through paid staff positions, a lie straight from hell.

Heavenly Father, thank you for your Unity. Make us One and keep us One as you are One. You in us and us in you. Thank you that you have placed your Son as The Head, we need only to hear and see and follow. Thank you for collective discernment, creative collaboration, participation with you by all of The Body parts and actions led by you that amaze and bring Joy. Teach us, Jesus; lead us, O Spirit; and do your works in us, Father!

Chapter Sixteen
A Case Study Comparison

While this chapter utilizing a church focus would appear to be irrelevant to for-profit organizations and non-profits, much is analogous and transferrable to the growth of any entity.

Over two decades ago I was cautioning a large church Individuated Director about his plan to hire staff for the upcoming completion of their new building. He anticipated going from a weekly attendance of 2,500 to 6,000 and a doubling of paid staff to 75% of budget. As I explained that I would like to show him a Connections process for adding 80% of the staff through the use of high-capacity non-paid leaders and the non-paid teams they would generate, he stopped me and said, "Volunteers don't show up. How are you going to control them?" Case closed.

What these people with a strong Director/weak Reconciler imbalance do not understand is that passionate people have a God-given purpose for which they show up. They are not showing up for you, though they may initially. If people find frustration in your Reconciler weakness and stop showing up, it is likely because you are draining their energy and sapping their commitment. Fulfilling God's passion within them provides payment in intrinsic reward, payment you cannot otherwise provide.

We don't need Leverage to Control anyone, we just need to prove to them that we are committed to Co-Leadership in Relational Mutually Accountable Co-Discipleship and that we will let them contribute – iron sharpening iron.

This church had been birthed with a God-given balance of alpha Directors and Reconcilers in leadership across the typical ministry areas. Unfortunately, this fast-growing Unity Operated church plant that grew through Leader Multiplication fell victim to Leader Replication. Having been advised by the leaders of their mentoring mega-church that it was OK to only hire people they "clicked with", they eventually collapsed on their

Director blind sides. (Years later, so did the Director of the mentoring church.)

This Director's career had been spent in the marketplace where the underlying risk of losing your job creates compliance. A founding member and visionary for the church plant, he initially tried to develop productive systems in the Unity OS using volunteer leaders. He was somewhat successful with Director leaders, but Reconciler leaders often left him as they continually experienced conflict in his Parallels OS (see Chapter Seven of *Life*) leadership style. (One reason why volunteers eventually stopped showing up.) Frustrated by his inability to *keep and Control* lead volunteers through Leverage – he began to hire staff as soon as giving levels would allow. Using Leader Replication, these leaders ran their ministries in a similar manner. Soon, staffing levels were through the roof and the need for money began to influence decision-making.

Some years later they had 6,000 in attendance and 80% of their huge budget going to payroll related expenses. They were the fastest growing church in the nation, but Individuated Leadership and Leader Replication had shielded them from the wise Correction God had been bringing through their opposites. Having hired so many "rubber stamps", what remained were a few Persevering alpha Reconcilers who were Rejected and discounted as Divisive.

In the years before their crash, Reconciler Idealists and Reconciler Guardians warned of the great financial risk while also recounting the relational damage that was occurring. Dismissively, they were told that they didn't have enough faith or that they just didn't "get it". Emboldened by the power of their growing Director imbalance, *Satan was crouching at these Directors' door.*

As much of the congregation was going through a Matthew 18 process, their mentoring church told them to select and place a Board of Elders over the staff and to begin using this new structure. This was the beginning of the Elder Takeover of the informal "staff of elders" that God had originally assimilated to birth and grow it. Giving the Director orders to lead more relationally, these new *formal* Elders took Authority hierarchically – Leveraging the Director. Do you see how *more* Power and Authority were the mentoring church's solution to their Power and Authority problem?

When we use Authority, Unity and the collective Wisdom offered to us by God are not our number one priority.

Utilizing their own individuated Authoritarian styles, Elder efforts were marginally effective. In one case a Director Elder even *opened* a one-on-one Matthew 18 meeting with a Reconciler by telling him that he should leave if he didn't like how things were being done. Impression-based Fundamental Attribution Errors and syllogistic Authority errors scuttled what could have been an insightful and cathartic time of understanding and healing. In the passionate area of faith, we find zealots trying to Control outcomes – and this new Hierarchical Organizational Structure of Elders>Board>Staff> fed into it.

The year the Global Financial Crisis hit they, like so very many other large churches, laid off dozens of staff. As it happened, the Elders held a meeting to notify the congregation that they were scaling things back to what they could Control. They confessed to previously having 80% of their budget going to paid staff and acknowledged knowing of congregations operating at 30%- 40%, but then shrugged and said that they didn't know how they were doing it.

When the TV News and local newspaper described the massive layoffs it was a huge embarrassment. Many wondered how a church could dump that many people into the unemployment line. Those headlines made it appear that God's church is no different than the businesses of the rest of the world. Unbelievers took note and firmed up their positions. God was not glorified by their actions! The following year attendance was down to 4,000 and attendance continued to dwindle for years. Overburdened financially, it eventually collapsed and was renamed.

Staff Are Sheep Too!

It's bad enough that this Director was unwilling to consider the suggestion. (As Pat Lencione said in his book The Advantage, we need to seek all of the input and gather all of the information if we are going to make informed decisions.) It's worse that so many staff had to scramble for jobs during the worst time to look for work since the Great Depression. What is saddest is that it didn't have to happen. Much of the money that for years was spent on staff could have went to *taking care of the widows and the orphans* of the broader community in such an attractive manner that they may have been at

10,000 due to better TV and newspaper coverage, God being glorified and many coming to faith during such difficult times.

If they had instead staffed up with non-paid alphas in Relational Mutually Accountable Co-Discipleship & Co-Leadership - paid staff at a 20%-30% budget level - there would not have been any staff layoffs during the Global Financial Crisis. And though *ministry* budgets may have required reductions, the *staff* and ministry teams would have still been available to serve in a community where so many had lost their jobs. This would have glorified God at a time when the headlines of huge staff layoffs would not!

It is not my interest to bring judgment to this, after all, most churches operate with a hierarchical Authority bias. Rather, my hope is that we would learn how they came to slide out of his Unity OS and into the hierarchical World OS – so that we might avoid doing so ourselves. This case study is not an isolated occurrence, it has happened in thousands of large church settings.

At startup, this church was a classic example of God's Unity Operating System thriving in a church plant. The Spirit led a high-capacity marketplace Director and a high-capacity Senior Pastor Reconciler to start a church that functioned in beautiful Unity, with brilliant teaching, worship and unbelievable transparency. The two were a perfect complementary match. (If you'd like to see their MBTI types, read *ENTJ* from page 231-240 of *Working Together* by Isachsen & Berens for the Director's type and read *INFP* from page 325-341 for the Reconciler's type.) Unaware of how God's Unity Operating System was at work among them, they didn't recognize that the World's Authoritarian Operating System was *crouching at the door* of their fast growth.

Unaware that much of their success was attributable to the cautionary relational pace of the Reconciler upon the speed of the Director, it became a huge point of ongoing conflict. The Director took the position typical to our World OS and lobbied for Individuated Authority so that he could lead where he "knew" they needed to grow.

Still, unaware of the value of the Reconciler's contribution to stability and Unity, we cannot blame the Director for wanting Individuated Authority. After all, it is commonly expected in the World OS/Parallels OS from which he came, so as to expedite productivity and the achievement of goals.

The beginning of the end of all that beautiful transparency and Unity came in a slow slide as he usurped control, growth accelerated, and he placed more and more Directors into paid leadership positions – adding more and more relational conflict.

Given their quickening pace and slowly crumbling relationship, the founding Director and Reconciler discontinued their daily communications of how each thought they should proceed. They kept busy leading their areas of individuated responsibility, no longer taking time to Authentically utilize their shared Visionary and Strategist giftedness and complementary Director and Reconciler giftedness. As they set aside team time one day each week in preparation for the next week, the Director would emphasize the execution he needed to those present – expecting the Reconciler to leave the details and pace of their overall Vision and Strategy to him. Weekly attendance and giving continued to rise while the fabric of staff relationships strained against the pressure.

What they said they were going to do during their weekly team meetings was sometimes not what really happened. The Director would then typically explain that he had had to make a Command decision in the moment to go another way and was sorry that there wasn't a way to communicate that and still make a decision in a timely way. Since we live in a culture that does not value Co-Leadership, who could blame the Director for *taking* the lead? In fact, in the hierarchical World OS, don't we expect it?

As we've seen, over time our organizations tend to look more and more like the lead leader. Advised by the mentoring church that he should hire people he "clicked with", the Director continued to hire and promote more Directors who would tend to agree with the Director's speed and direction. Also unaware that it would be a problem, over time the Reconciler was worn down by the many D's and was no longer able to influence their productivity focused arguments in favor of Relational integrity. Over time, other Reconcilers went quiet or just left. Conflict seemed natural and unavoidable to the imbalanced Director majority since having winners and losers is just a part of life (in the World OS where they were trained).

The remaining alpha Reconcilers began stepping forward to warn that Relational issues were occurring far too frequently. As you might imagine, the imbalanced staff felt appropriately concerned by Reconciler input, but not responsible. After all, they Rationalized, these Reconcilers simply didn't understand the difficulty of their position. "The responsibility of leadership to provide steerage and the Driving of execution in such times requires Speed and agility. Conflict is unfortunately part of the process. Some people just don't get it!"

Still making Fundamental Attribution Errors, syllogistic Authority errors and lacking in personality assessment skills, most staff disagreed with and disrespected their Reconciler Disruptors - further increasing the Relational distance between them. Typical to the cycle below, as people began choosing sides, they necessarily searched for a more tenable position.

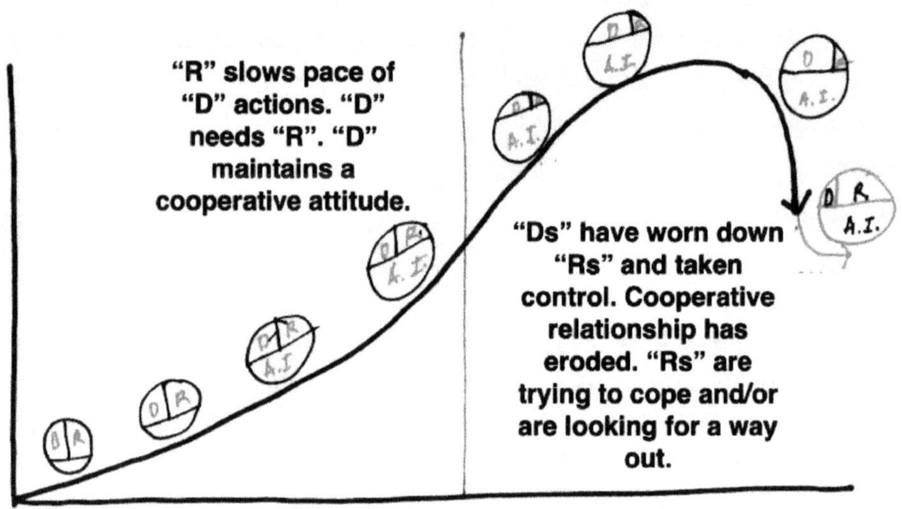

The Authoritarian World Operating System fails us fundamentally, especially at scale, because we no longer know each other.

Unfortunately, sides remained due to the Elders' use of the Parallels OS, and many a Reconciler left the church shaking their head in disbelief. Other illuminating elements of this case study are included elsewhere in this book according to topical content, but suffice it to say that the Director eventually had to leave. His replacement, said to be a conciliator, struggled under his own opaque Individuated Leadership. (If you'd like to see his MBTI type, read *INTJ* from page 241-251 of *Working Together* by Isachsen & Berens.)

As with the Director who had to leave, he operated under Elders who continued oversight with a dependence upon the Parallels OS, Hierarchy, Individuated Leadership, Spiritual Gifts and an old and ineffective MBTI understanding. Still unaware of the wealth of facilitative personality science also at their disposal, the Elders and leaders remained protective and opaque, much like Oz hiding behind the curtain of their Authority. Their mantra became, "If you want to go fast, go alone. But if you want to go far, go together." Trained in the Authoritarian World OS, they did not realize that, foundationally, nothing had really changed. In classic style, they eventually fired their new Reconciler for lack of productivity.

It is unfortunately quite common for churches to cycle back and forth in their individuated Parallels Operating Systems from Director leadership to Reconciler leadership – a teeter-totter like ride that often includes a decade or more between the changes.

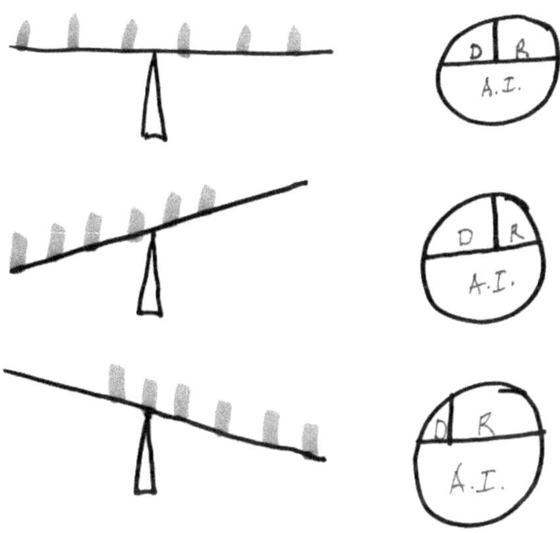

The graphic above describes the evolution of an initially balanced Unity Operating System church plant that grows in scale. Reacting to the natural tendencies of Directors to assume control over time, note that the Director is eventually replaced with a Reconciler so as to restore Unity. It would not be surprising years later to find, as we did with our example church above, that the individuated Reconciler has been judged as unproductive and replaced with yet another individuated Director.

As we will see in the alternate Case Study, balanced D+R "Staff Are The Elders" Teams may be sustained for many decades.

A Striking Comparison

While the church described above was teeter-tottering through its third split in 25 years, the following church has been without a split for more than 40 years. Birthed in a nearly identical fashion, the founders are now retiring and have begun the seamless transition identified several years ago. The key difference? The Unity Operating System and the "Staff Are The Elders" flat Organizational Structure, with Christ as the Head!

As this church was being birthed, church plant mentors told the pastor to set himself up in CEO style. However, his ear for God's voice and his knowledge of the scriptures told him to do otherwise. In the same way that God birthed the above-described church, a balance of alpha Directors and Reconcilers found leadership roles in the standard areas. While the Director above had a view of the future wherein hierarchical Authority would emerge, this church took the position that *collective wisdom* under God's Authority was all they would need. That, and eyes that see and ears that hear - collectively.

They saw a future where they would never cease to collectively discern the will of the Father with the founding staff as Elders. Never cease in asking him for his Direction and never cease in keeping Relational Unity primary over productivity. More than good sounding policy, they lived it. And grew!

Though the Enemy came at them at every turn, Unity came to the rescue each time. They were indivisible, even while iron sharpened iron. They added alpha leaders in Mutually Accountable Co-Leadership and Co-Discipleship as the years went by, and the church became one of the largest around.

This model church plant prepared for growth spurts through an alpha leader development process modelling Co-Leadership and Co-Discipleship in Relational Mutual Accountability. As they added additional alphas from within, they found expanded vision and grew Staff Eldership to include a portion of the new staff - a total of twelve. Each were deeply involved in day-to-day ministry – some paid, some unpaid – developing and maintaining strong relationships along the way.

Paid staff size remained small in comparison with most churches, a great percentage of The Whole Body was engaged and Jesus' commands to Love were evident to the surrounding community. When the Global Financial Crisis hit there were no layoffs, though there were *budget* reductions.

As ministry expanded, they have always had alphas ready to take on the Co-Leadership challenges – unpaid. For decades they have operated an internship program that draws future leaders into ministry for mentoring.

There were no layoffs during the COVID-19 epidemic either, and they took full advantage of the opportunity by blessing the surrounding community each week with huge food giveaways. God was honored as many of the needy committed or recommitted themselves in fresh faith. This is Love!

Love one another: just as I have loved you, you also are to love one another.
By this all people will know that you are my talmidim,
if you have love for one another.

The Enemy could not point to hypocrisy in this church during the Global Financial Crisis or COVID-19 epidemic. Rather, God was glorified as the community saw the great impact they were making on behalf of those in need. Leadership was United, iron sharpened iron and God was further glorified as some of the served came in and were saved!

As they prepared to enter their 4th decade, they realized that the younger staff had *become* ready to transition into greater leadership: Eldership. They had lived in Unity together according to what Jesus had said, "…*their* leaders exercise Authority over them. But it shall not be so among *you*." Having lived in it, they know how to continue it.

The slow transition of elder Elders retiring and younger Elders coming in is going well, and is being well received by The Body. Flat organizational structures, void of Authority based action, bring Unity of action, longevity of Unity and a future beyond what we could ever dream, hope or imagine.

As the previously discussed church went through their first split, they placed a hierarchy of Elders above in supervision. Like in the book Animal Farm, they went from the Unity OS into a Parallels OS. As they became more and more Authority based according to the pervasive hierarchical Military Chain Of Command Culture, the founding staff came under Leverage – and began *Self-Selecting* their way out.

In the Unity Operating System church plant, the founding staff are the Elders and stay the Elders as they scale. Elders, additional staff and congregants all reside on the same hierarchical plane in a flat org chart under Christ as the Head. All are in Relational Mutually Accountable Co-Discipleship always. All Advise. Transparent, leaders are more likely to remain humble, gaining greater maturity and Christ-likeness as they age. Alphas are found as with the shepherd boy David while Samuel was looking for the next king. In these, Collective Wisdom discerns the Mind of Christ and talmidim are developed and grow in leadership maturity. In these, his kingdom continues to come on earth as it is in heaven, glory by glory, as each are conformed more and more into the image of our Creator.

I should note here an interesting approach to the development of elder leadership. You might consider *doubling up* elders into Co-Leadership Teams of 24 such that 12 older elders mentor and co-lead with12 younger elders-in-training. While some of the younger 12 may eventually become Elders, others, benefitting from the experience, may go on to plant new churches elsewhere in God's Unity Operating System and Structure. We'll take a look at Structure in Chapter Seventeen.

Chapter Seventeen

Lessons Learned

Maintain Balance While Scaling Up

Over time the ratio between the number of leaders and the number of those in the seats may shift dramatically. True for any congregation, entity or community, let's continue to think of it in terms of the church plant. We might represent the earlier ratio and the later ratio this way:

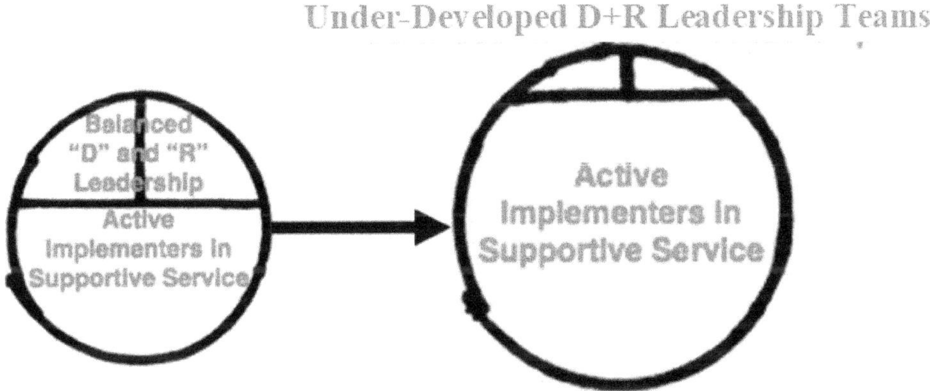

As church plants, given the clear need for leaders and the scarcity of funds, Unity OS Advice from God's alpha Advisors (Encouragers, Correctors and Disrupters) was necessarily considered. As church plants, motivated by our need for leaders, we would Connect quickly with these alphas and invite them into Mutually Accountable non-paid Co-Leadership roles. In Christ-like leadership development, we were able to release them to *greater things* with us together in Co-Leadership - and thanked God for uniting them with us! It was not complicated; it just took time to build trust in the Co-Discipled relationship!

Unfortunately, as we scale the ratio between Leaders and Active Implementers in Supportive Service may broaden. Over time, with under-developed D+R Co-Leadership growth, the *active* make up only 55% of the congregation – with the inactive 45% still badly in need of life-on-life relationship and involvement! This is where leader stress builds and the yoke *becomes* so very heavy. In-fighting develops under the strain, and is the relational breaking point between us, us and our congregants, and between us and our families as our worktime requirements extend! This is when the slippery slope for Directors to *take over* as CEOs/Commanders becomes most tempting! Don't miss your chance at balanced D+R development!

We need to have a preparatory view for developing broad un-paid alpha leadership early on and always! We cannot scale and allow our leader/server ratios to change – as we try to maintain Control. The only way to accomplish it is with the ongoing alpha leader development mentioned previously, trusting God to bring *who* we need in preparation *before* we need them.

Brainstorm Placeholders

When we were a small church plant, most people had a somewhat aligned degree of vision for what was going to be needed in the future because we came from church backgrounds. It's not too difficult to have vision when history has been instructive, however, as we scale up, leaders tend to stop developing leaders *in advance* for future needs because of insufficient funds. We tend to dismiss some of our God-given alpha visionaries just when we need them most – in *preparation* for *the plans he has for us*.

Whether idealistic or practical, any vision that cannot be identified as a bad thing should find placeholder status for potential future implementation – and be advertised (as will be described) so as to request those passionate for it to come forward to eventually birth it. Otherwise, how might any alpha who *would* agree with the vision ever find their way to *joining* us in *preparation* for it?

When we transparently identify the potential for large future needs early, we are better able to brainstorm a development process with our congregations far in advance, saving money for *the widows and the orphans*. When leaders operate with transparency, the creation of placeholders helps the alphas in our midst to contemplate our future together synergistically. In this way every dreamer has a place to put their dream, whether or not Active Implementers are ready to Unite around them.

When we allow dreamers an outlet for sharing their vision throughout the congregation, we effectively offer others opportunity to raise their own hands and say, "Me, too! I'll help!" - or wait patiently until more do. This never happens utilizing the World OS or Parallels OS because we always wait to initiate until we have funds available to hire staff, and therefore retain the ability to use Leverage as a *MANagement* tool.

In the young church plant, leaders would come up after service, introduce themselves and make an offer to contribute. These Leaders Out Of Nowhere were gifts from God for the plans he had for us. Needing everyone, we invited them in and they became extremely important parts of The Body.

As we scale, we tend to hold these people at arm's length, perhaps Rejecting the very people God is continuing to send. Moses was initially a Rejected Leader Out Of Nowhere. Jesus was a Rejected Leader Out Of Nowhere. Our Father sends *us* Leaders Out Of Nowhere, too. The elders were the first to Reject Moses and Jesus. Are you Rejecting, too?

Returning to the old way we used as church plants, we facilitate meaningful ligamental Connections between those of similar passion to come to know each other - and potentially bring dreams to reality way ahead of *our* schedule and according to *his*. We otherwise make it more likely that God's minor prophets, visionaries and Leaders Out Of Nowhere never have the chance to contribute.

Sample Adonai-ical Decision-Making Process:
It is common process for us to define a problem, propose solution options, select a solution and then move on to implementing the solution. However, it works differently in the Unity OS. For example, I might see fit to put on my Director hat, direct the Group's or Team's attention to an issue and provide a possible solution: "It seems to me that the way forward in solving this problem might just be for us to….."

Then, having heard the thoughts of the Director, we *all* put on our Reconciler hats (including me) and begin to add our thoughts: "OK, I see what you are getting at. That could work, but we might want to consider revising it to include……"

Once all have spoken and a revised solution seems to have taken shape, we ask if we have all Reconciled our positions to it together. If so, we move to the next step. If not, it will be because someone is Directing our attention to what seems to have been overlooked. We must then consider whether or not we can Reconcile ourselves to *this* information, and continue the process until we have all Reconciled ourselves to the *same* position. This is the big difference between the World OS and the Unity OS. In the Unity OS we take the time needed to include every area of disagreement and work through each respectfully. (Please see the caveat below.) In the World OS, we would get to the point of a solid majority and then vote so as to be expedient - politics! Voting that allows for winners and losers breeds Division!

In the Unity OS, we take as much time as is needed, even if it requires many meetings over a long period of time.

Once we have all Reconciled ourselves to the same position, it is time to Actively Implement the solution. At this point, we must all *take off our Director and Reconciler hats with regard to the solution* and then put them back on again *with regard to implementation.* As we discuss who might be best for which portions of the solution, we utilize the same process to determine *who* will implement which portions. Once this has been accomplished, we all put on our Active Implementer hats and take action in Unity.

Caveat

As you prayerfully consider adding a co-leader into any leadership role, remember that your value for unanimity in decision-making may be at risk. Is this person truly ready? Clearly, we must move cautiously when considering new team member invitations. Since a single person can stall a decision for all of us, we must be certain that this person has been "sent by God". We must not only discern that it was God who provided us their talent, resources and expertise, but that we have appropriately considered this person prayerfully and for an appropriately long period of time. Proof of an understanding of what the Unity OS truly looks like, and of the Values and Structure it utilizes, are critical.

This is also when we must take great care with regard to our tendencies to want to be Gate Keepers. Could it be that some are saying that "they are not yet ready" because they are our D or R or personality opposites? Rejecting them so as to "protect" the integrity of "our" entity is an oft made mistake. To some extent we may say that <u>none of us</u> are really and truly ready!

Perhaps the qualifying question is: "Are they a sincere talmid as evidenced by posture and humility in Jesus' attitudes of the Beatitudes with fruit of the Spirit language and actions?"

Is he/she truly being led by God?

The Enemy would love to insert a well-intentioned person into leadership who he may occasionally mislead so as to disrupt, slow or altogether stop what God is leading the rest of leadership to do. Since it is possible for any one individual to stall a decision through their singular disagreement, we must move cautiously before adding a leader in Co-Leadership. Ongoing attention to divisive tendencies must lead to Relational Mutually Accountable Co-Discipleship such that we *participate* with God in his sanctification of them (and us). Those who reject it are simply not ready. Remember Henry Cloud's previously mentioned teaching on the Wise, the Fool and the Evil and respond appropriately.

I have seen the opposite of this issue, as well, when one who was truly being prompted to raise the stop/pause sign was ignored and a vote taken so as to move on expeditiously. Later, after it was too late and that singular person was found to be correct, the damage was done, conflict exacerbated, and Unity further diminished. I say *further diminished*, because it could only be through some level of disunity that resorting to politics and the use of voting can occur.

In Summary

May the wise acknowledge the character of God, the revelation in his Word, the leading of the Holy Spirit, the Authority Deception of the Enemy, the rationalizations of mankind, the needs of the widow and the orphan, facilitative scientific data on our Triune personal tendencies and our learnings from observing his Unity OS, the World OS and the Parallels OS.

Typically, church ministry is dependent upon the leadership of paid staff at a cost of roughly 50% of our budgets. We need to overhaul our operating systems and structure to make room for *all* of the paid and non-paid leadership giftedness if we will leave more for *the widows and the orphans*. When we are in Relational Mutual Accountability and Co-Discipleship with our alpha Directors and Reconcilers, our mutual sanctification and maturation will allow us to Co-Lead ministry with as little as 20%-30% paid staff. This is far more responsible to paid staff, as well, in that future economic downturns should not cause them to be laid off.

As our church plants grow, let us take great care in discerning if and when to hire alpha tent makers. Unpaid alpha Co-Leaders may easily lead ministries of non-paid Supportive Servers and eventually find their way into

Elder roles. If we really desire excellence, let them Co-Lead and contribute to Elder discussions. Yes, they will be a challenge, but they will also be a blessing and that's why God brought them to you!

It is very likely that Jehovah Jireh has already provided you with more high-capacity leaders than you probably now have in paid staff! We are the biggest obstacles to engaging the currently inactive Active Implementers in Supportive Service because we are unwilling to do the hard work of leadership: transparent facilitative Relational Mutually Accountable Co-Discipleship with high-capacity alphas in Co-Leadership service that engages the inactive.

National surveys have found that an average of 45% of the people in any given church are inactive. According to scientific personality data, that would typically mean that 6%-10% of those are high-capacity leaders. That would mean that 3%-5% of the remaining inactive are high-capacity alphas. If your weekly attendance is 100, you have 3-5 latent high-capacity alphas to identify, co-disciple with and facilitate to active service leading Supportive Servers in Active Implementation. If you have 1000 in weekly attendance, that would be 30-50 latent high-capacity alphas. We need to be identifying the remaining 3%-5% of inactive Directors and Reconcilers for Leadership Development.

Many successfully provide such targeted Relational Mutually Accountable Co-Discipleship for their tent-making high-capacity alpha leaders with yearlong groups of 10-20 people each. If leadership will avail themselves in the Small Group environment and get to know alphas individually, by the end of the year everyone will know what everyone else is passionate about leading, have worked a process with them to identify their Co-Leaders and have begun inviting Active Implementers to join them through one of the many facilitative Connections Team processes.

At scale, it is easier to make FAEs and so miss Connecting with our supportive alpha (Encourager/Corrector/Disruptor) Advisory opportunities. In the ways of the world there can only be one boss so we label alphas and avoid them - and it's much easier than initiating a relationship. These assumptions allow us to rationalize separation, and cause us to lose the synergy we could have gained. At scale, and somewhat comfortable due to the number of paid staff *under* us, it is easier to describe a scarcity of time and not get to know them. We are, therefore, the ones who relegate them to the 45% inactive.

These are obviously people with a passion for something, and might just be a Leader Out Of Nowhere, now here! Ask them into an Advisory Forum process to better understand them and determine next steps. That's what we did when we were a small church plant. We need an assimilation process like we used then. There *are* next steps for everyone, there must be. They are a portion of The Body of Christ.

"The role of the leader is to equip/prepare/facilitate the people to acts of service."

These are otherwise opportunities lost, and the bigger the church the greater the likelihood that they feel rejected by you. Have you ever done a survey asking your people to tell you how easy or hard it is to find their ministry fit with you? Consider what one high-capacity alpha said, "You have rejected what God gave me to contribute." Though we *may* not mean to be saying, "We don't need you." it might just be the very message we are sending.

Unless there is a Relational Mutually Accountable purpose-filled Co-Discipleship/Co-Leadership Development process - we likely will not integrate them. We need Co-Discipleship/Co-Leadership development tracks if we really want them to Connect productively and sustainably. God has given us a great many high-capacity leaders and supportive servers because we need them - we cannot rationalize away the reality that we are to find ways for all to be able to serve together! Once we set aside our hierarchical Authority mind set and instead describe a Co-Led Co-Discipled path in oneness – we will find ourselves in a very workable 5 Step environment:

1. *Identify and invite the remaining 3%-5% of inactive alpha Directors and Reconcilers for Leadership Development.*
2. *Learn what each person is passionate about leading and why.*
3. *In the Spirit of talmidim, provide targeted Relational Mutually Accountable Co-Discipleship for these tent-making high-capacity alpha leaders in a Leadership Development small group. Include opportunities*

for each to fully explain and clarify their Advice and ministry leadership ideas.

4. *Avail yourself transparently in the small group environment. Go out with them individually and get to know each personally. Perhaps give them copies of Life, Love and Leading (They're free upon request!) and meet with them each week to talk through what they have read.*
5. *Work a process to identify their passion-aligned Co-Leaders and then begin inviting Active Implementers to join them through one of the many facilitative Connections processes.*

Thank you, El Shaddai, that everything we need to do everything you have given us is being resourced by you. You are the best boss of all time! When we look around and come to believe that we do not have everything we need, help us to remember that our pace and our productivity come through you. Help us to see who and what we are missing, what we are to do and where we are to do it – in your timing. May we not get ahead of you, become anxious in identifying resources on our own and fall into the Enemy's traps. Thank you that your yoke is easy and your burden is light. Help me to know that which is mine to do and that which is not. May I not invade the space of those you have selected for the very efforts I am considering on my own. Teach me, O Jesus; Lead me, O Spirit; Do your works in me, O Father!

Chapter Eighteen

Participating In *His* Administration

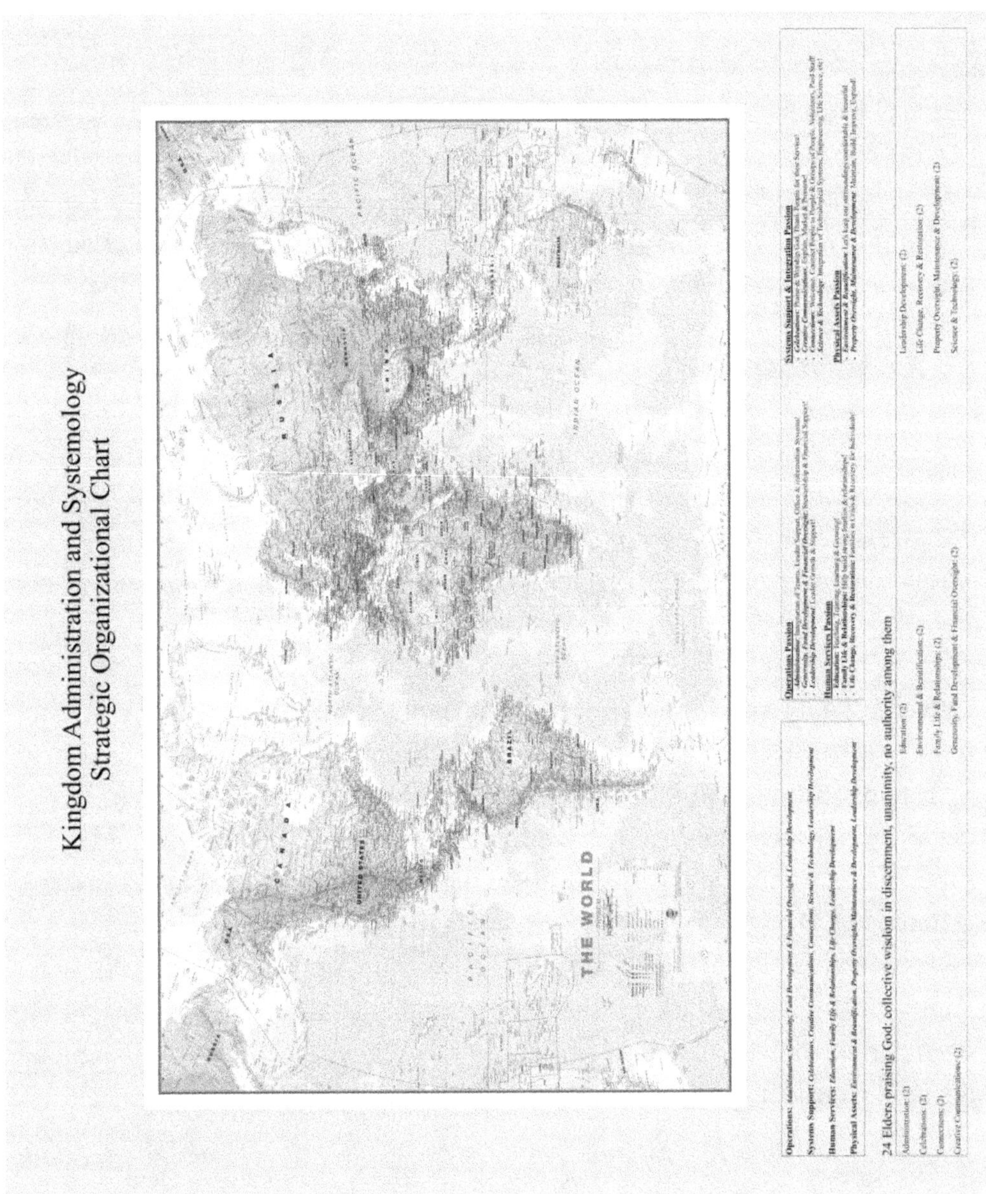

Multiple Old Testament passages share the deep faith and trust that David had in God. David's intimate relationship with God was such that he was often found singing to him in praise and thanksgiving. In 1 Samuel 23, we see him approach the throne of grace with confidence, inquiring conversationally of the Lord God who knows all things real and possible. In right relationship, God responded to David with the information needed simply because he asked. Through the conversation, his best choice became clear, though it is not one of the potentialities he asked about:

1 Samuel 23:8-13

8 And Saul summoned all the people to war, to go down to Keilah, to besiege David and his men. 9 David knew that Saul was plotting harm against him. And he said to Abiathar the priest, "Bring the ephod here." 10 Then David said, "O Lord, the God of Israel, your servant has surely heard that Saul seeks to come to Keilah, to destroy the city on my account. 11 Will the men of Keilah surrender me into his hand? Will Saul come down, as your servant has heard? O Lord, the God of Israel, please tell your servant." And the Lord said, "He will come down." 12 Then David said, "Will the men of Keilah surrender me and my men into the hand of Saul?" And the Lord said, "They will surrender you." 13 Then David and his men, who were about six hundred, arose and departed from Keilah, and they went wherever they could go. When Saul was told that David had escaped from Keilah, he gave up the expedition.

Neither did Saul come down, nor the people of Keilah surrender David to him. This because David knew what would happen if he stayed. So he left.

Having just rescued Keilah from the Philistines, David could have decided on his own to stay with the logical expectation that they would support him when Saul arrived. Instead, he asked of God, and it made all the difference.

As described in Chapter Six of the *Life* section, in (Genesis 2:19-20, 1 Kings 22:19-23 and Mark 6:34-44) we learn that God offers *willing participants* of his kingdom *creative collaboration* in the accomplishment of his will. Consider our *first creative participation* with him:

Genesis 2:19-20

19 Now out of the ground the Lord God had formed every beast of the field and every bird of the heavens and brought them to the man to see what he would call them. And whatever the man called every living creature, that was its name. 20 The man gave names to all livestock and to the birds of the heavens and to every beast of the field...

Adam participated with him then, and later the disciples participated with him as well. Jesus didn't do it alone:

Mark 6:34-44

34 When he went ashore he saw a great crowd, and he had compassion on them, because they were like sheep without a shepherd. And he began to teach them many things. 35 And when it grew late, his disciples came to him and said, "This is a desolate place, and the hour is now late. 36 Send them away to go into the surrounding countryside and villages and buy themselves something to eat." 37 But he answered them, "You give them something to eat." And they said to him, "Shall we go and buy two hundred denarii worth of bread and give it to them to eat?" 38 And he said to them, "How many loaves do you have? Go and see." And when they had found out, they said, "Five, and two fish." 39 Then he commanded them all to sit down in groups on the green grass. 40 So they sat down in groups, by hundreds and by fifties. 41 And taking the five loaves and the two fish, he looked up to heaven and said a blessing and broke the loaves and gave them to the disciples to set before the people. And he divided the two fish among them all. 42 And they all ate and were satisfied. 43 And they took up twelve baskets full of broken pieces and of the fish. 44 And those who ate the loaves were five thousand men.

It is his joy that, made in his own creative image, we might creatively imagine ways and means for accomplishment. We are invited to participate *in his will*, even while he allows us to be creative *with him* insofar as *how* it might be accomplished. He does not desire robots following orders.

The meeting 1 Kings 22 records clearly defines it to be a portion of his heavenly administration. Paraphrasing, God says that he will intervene to deliver his people from evil – from King Ahab. As he shares *his will*, he asks for ways that it might be done. Finally, he chooses one of them and says that it will be done *that way*, and successfully so.

1 Kings 22:19-23

19 And Micaiah said, "Therefore hear the word of the Lord: I saw the Lord sitting on his throne, and all the host of heaven standing beside him on his right hand and on his left; 20 and the Lord said, 'Who will entice Ahab, that he may go up and fall at Ramoth-gilead?' And one said one thing, and another said another. 21 Then a spirit came forward and stood before the Lord, saying, 'I will entice him.' 22 And the Lord said to him, 'By what means?' And he said, 'I will go out, and will be a lying spirit in the mouth of all his prophets.' And he said, 'You are to entice him, and you shall succeed; go out and do so.' 23 Now therefore behold, the Lord has put a lying spirit in the mouth of all these your prophets; the Lord has declared disaster for you."

Both the Old Testament and New Testament writers help us see that this activity is to be true for us here and now as well, and that it will continue to be so forever after Jesus' return. If we will *participate* with him *in his will* on earth as it is in heaven *now*, we will also participate with him on the *new* earth after he comes again:

Matthew 19:28-29

28 Jesus said to them, "Truly, I say to you, in the new world, when the Son of Man will sit on his glorious throne, you who have followed me will also sit on twelve thrones, judging the twelve tribes of Israel. 29 And everyone who has left houses or brothers or sisters or father or mother or children or lands, for my name's sake, will receive a hundredfold and will inherit eternal life.

1 Corinthians 6:2-3a

2 Or do you not know that the saints will judge the world? And if the world is to be judged by you, are you incompetent to try trivial cases? 3 Do you not know that we are to judge angels?

2 Timothy 2:12

if we endure, we will also reign with him; if we deny him, he also will deny us;

Revelation 2:26

The one who conquers and who keeps my works until the end, to him I will give authority over the nations,

Revelation 3:21

The one who conquers, I will grant him to sit with me on my throne, as I also conquered and sat down with my Father on his throne.

Revelation 20:6

6 Blessed and holy is the one who shares in the first resurrection! Over such the second death has no power, but they will be priests of God and of Christ, and they will reign with him for a thousand years.

Revelation 21:1

Then I saw a new heaven and a new earth, for the first heaven and the first earth had passed away, and the sea was no more.

Revelation 22:5

And night will be no more. They will need no light of lamp or sun, for the Lord God will be their light, and they will reign forever and ever.

In 1 Corinthians 6 above, Paul reminds us that we should be about participating in God's business here and now. Jesus himself shows us a portion of this administrative participation in Revelation 4. This is supported in Daniel 4, Daniel 7, Isaiah 6, Ezekiel 1-11 and other portions of the New Testament.

Revelation 4:1-4

After this I looked, and behold, a door standing open in heaven! And the first voice, which I had heard speaking to me like a trumpet, said, "Come up here, and I will show you what must take place after this." 2 At once I was in the Spirit, and behold, a throne stood in heaven, with one seated on the throne. 3 And he who sat there had the appearance of jasper and carnelian, and around the throne was a rainbow that had the appearance of an emerald. 4 Around the throne were twenty-four thrones, and seated on the thrones were twenty-four elders, clothed in white garments, with golden crowns on their heads.

Mark 1:14-15

14 Now after John was arrested, Jesus came into Galilee, proclaiming the gospel of God, 15 and saying, "The time is fulfilled, and the kingdom of God is at hand; repent and believe in the gospel."

Matthew 12:25-28

25 Knowing their thoughts, he said to them, "Every kingdom divided against itself is laid waste, and no city or house divided against itself will stand. 26 And if Satan casts out Satan, he is divided against himself. How then will his kingdom stand? 27 And if I cast out demons by Beelzebul, by whom do your sons cast them out? Therefore they will be your judges. 28 But if it is by the Spirit of God that I cast out demons, then the kingdom of God has come upon you.

****

The kingdom of God has come upon you.
What does its organizational structure look like?

If God is administering his Kingdom (and he is), how many *departments* or *ministries* does he utilize? This is important! *If we are to be administering his Kingdom with him, would it not be helpful to know how he has structured them?* How many ministries do we require? How can we know that, structurally, we are functioning to administer utilizing all of his groupings?

Physical things have a completeness, or lack thereof, that may be seen. Not so for the invisible. The consultant in me long ago started asking God to identify for me invisible System and Structure that my work might be *wholistic*.

If I do not have two arms, I cannot be as *physically* effective as if I were *whole*.

If your body has a marginally functioning internal organ I cannot know it, though evidentially I may be able to identify that you are somehow weaker than I would expect. Still, I cannot see which organ is the cause.

Structurally speaking, Spiritually speaking, how do you know if your *organization* is whole? If my organization is missing any portion of its *invisible structure*, how might I know? Evidentially there would be weakness, potholes that we continue to fall into, so to speak.

As I began to ask God about this 25 years ago, he began to help me *see*. I began taking note of the typical potholes and began looking for the ways that they would repeat. In doing so, I was able to identify the uniqueness of the successes in others who had avoided them. As I did this, I heard their comments and explanations and began to see that their *vision* for the *invisible* was far different than most - so I began categorizing these successes. Cumulatively, a combined vision for what consistently succeeded in an assortment of these issues began to fall into place in inter-related *administrative* categories and groups.

One of the benefits of consulting is the opportunity to probe deep inside the operations of others, identify the successes unique to them and pass the learnings along to future clients. As I asked God to identify the number of ministries in his administration, I also needed to ask him to give me usable names for each. As he walked me through my homework; churches, corporations and individuals allowed me deep into their lives to further sort it out. That, of course, brought more questions, and with the answers came the breakdown of these groups into categories that we all would commonly call Teams. But how accurate *were* my Groups and Teams?

Over the last 20 years I have been sharing my findings with many many others for their consideration. As the collective wisdom of so many others was assimilated, I would share the refinements with the folks who had contributed previously. Over the years, with the collective wisdom God has provided, I have come to believe that the number of ministries/departments/segments/categories/teams in any given *whole* life or entity is twelve, and that these derive from four Groups. Even at scale.

For much of our history, the entire USA has been administered by a Team of 12 Cabinet positions. Switzerland uses seven Ministry Teams for the administration of their country. How many is God using? How many do I need personally? How many does an organization need? As far as I can discern, the answer for *wholeness* in *every* case is twelve. If any of these are missing or in some way limited, maximal productivity will not occur. Less than *whole*, maximal productivity simply *cannot* occur.

- **Operations Group**
  - Administration Team
    - Integration of Teams, Leader Support, Office & Information Systems!
  - Generosity, Fund Development & Financial Oversight Team
    - Stewardship & Financial Support!
  - Leadership Development Team
    - Leader Growth & Support!

- **Systems Support & Integration Group**
  - Celebrations Team
    - Praise & Worship God, Thank People for their Service!
  - Creative Communications Team
    - Explain, Market & Promote!
  - Connections Team
    - Welcome People, Connect People & Groups of People, Volunteers, Paid Staff!
  - Science & Technology Team
    - Integration of Technological Systems, Engineering, Life Science, etc!
- **Human Services Group**
  - Education Team
    - Teaching, Training, Learning & Growing!
  - Family Life & Relationships Team
    - Help build strong families & relationships!
  - Life Change, Recovery & Restoration Team
    - Families in Crisis & Recovery for Individuals!
- **Physical Assets Group**
  - Environment & Beautification Team
    - Let's keep our surroundings comfortable & beautiful!
  - Property Oversight, Maintenance & Development Team
    - Maintain, Build, Improve, Expand!

Whether or not I am accurate as to whether the number of Teams is twelve, the important thing to consider is our difficulty with envisioning the abstract whole. Some will want to immediately begin to scrutinize the above Groups and Teams, and by all means go ahead! Just make sure that you ask God to help you see and find wholeness with a heart after his. Any consideration of this kind should not be about who is right, but must be about how we may better support each other as we live, work and play together! Until we align the people of our churches structurally across our communities for our communities, we will always lack the synergy that aligned One Kingdom Unity would otherwise bring.

If your org chart has been created according to individual staff roles, it is critically important that you abandon that system! As I have often seen, organizational charts that are laid out by *staff position* create Authoritarian silos that block the flow of information *between* Teams. Regarding churches, they also make it extremely difficult for the Parts of The Body sitting in the seats to find their fit because they are being pointed to a *person with a purpose* to lead them rather than *their own passionate God-given purpose.* These structures tend toward systems where Leadership Replication occurs rather than Leadership Multiplication, the inflow of Advisory information is blocked by Gate Keepers, and the diverse Connections Culture becomes a Selections Culture espousing conformity – and that leads to *more* Leader Replication.

When we use Authority, Unity and the collective Wisdom offered to us by God are not our number one priority.

We are committed to:

- One-ness: Him in us and us in Him
- Acts of Love & Intercession
- Hearts after the Father in attitudes consistent with the Beatitudes: Jesus' attitudes
- Fruit of the Spirit Language & Actions
- Connecting & Inviting
- Relational Mutually Accountable Co-Discipleship
- Development of Balanced Director/Reconciler Teams in Co-Leadership
- Leadership Teams that Do Not Have or Use Hierarchy/Authority
- Unity/Unanimity in Decisions & Actions
- Groups of Teams and Teams of Groups
- Leadership Development at All Levels
- Advisory Forums at ALL levels
  - *Collective* discernment of the Input of ALL People
  - Has God brought us a Leader Out Of Nowhere, now here?
- Facilitating Spirit-Led Self-Selection of Service

God, who is able to scale himself down to touch the individual, also scales himself up to avail his administration of the entire universe of physical and spiritual beings – all at the same time! He is the same yesterday, today and tomorrow. He never changes at any scale! Below are the same Groups and Teams as above, with descriptions to help us consider them with regard to our own *personal* wholeness:

Developing Personal Wholeness as God Grows Me

- **My Operations**
  - Administration
    - Creation of Income and Compliance with Laws, Banking & Information Systems
  - Generosity & Financial
    - Giving where God Leads me to Give; Strengthening my Financial Situation
  - Leadership Development
    - Grow my Leadership Ability & Support those I Lead
- **My Human Service**
  - Education
    - Learning & Growing; Teaching & Training
  - Family Life & Relationships
    - Strengthening and Growing in my Love and Care for Others
  - Life Change, Recovery & Restoration
    - Overcoming my Personal Issues; Strengthening People in Crisis & Recovery
- **My Relationships Support & Integration**
  - Celebrate
    - Praise & Worship God for What He Is Doing, Thank People for their Service
  - Creatively Communicate
    - Explain, Share & Promote the Advancement of the Kingdom of God
  - Connect
    - Welcome People; Connect with People; Connect People with Other People; Connect Groups of People
  - Science & Technology
    - Utilize Technology, Understand Life Science, be Attentive to my Health
- **My Physical Assets**
  - Environment & Beautification
    - Let's Keep our Surroundings Comfortable & Beautiful
  - Property Oversight, Maintenance & Development
    - Take Good Care of What I Have, Build, Repair, Improve, Expand

When we consider the totality of what it means to be talmidim *together*, we have a full complement of reminders that may be placed on the walls in our meeting rooms and wherever else we may desire to be able to quickly look to them for reference - *as iron sharpens iron* among us. In this way, we are personally able to consider ourselves and any entity in One-ness, as taught by Jesus, led by the Holy Spirit and in agreement with the Father in us doing his works – asking as in the prayer Jesus taught us, in agreement with all of John 17 and that he send more laborers!

We are committed to:

- One-ness: Him in us and us in Him
- His Unity Operating System and Structure for The Body
- Personal Wholeness
- Hearts after the Father in attitudes consistent with the Beatitudes: Jesus' attitudes
- Fruit of the Spirit Language & Actions
- Acts of Love & Intercession
- Connecting & Inviting
- Relational Mutually Accountable Co-Discipleship
- Development of Balanced Director/Reconciler Teams in Co-Leadership
- Leadership Teams that Do Not Have or Use Hierarchy/Authority
- Unity/Unanimity in Decisions & Actions
- Groups of Teams and Teams of Groups
- Leadership Development at All Levels
- Advisory Forums at ALL levels
  - *Collective* discernment of the Input of ALL People
  - Has God brought us a Leader Out Of Nowhere, now here?
- Facilitating Spirit-Led Self-Selection of Service

Developing Personal Wholeness & Holiness as God Grows Me

On our path to godliness

Unity Builders: In Humility & Love *The Spirit of the Lord offers freedom, so we:*		**Unity Busters: In Fear of Loss** *In our attempt to Control, we:*
◊ Inform with Gentleness	←	◊ Accuse, Judge, Condemn to Justify our Demands
◊ Encourage with Kindness	←	◊ Use Blame, Anger and Malice to Threaten and Coerce
◊ Explain with grace in Peace	←	◊ Use Shame & Silence to subtly Threaten Abandonment
◊ Share with compassion in Goodness	←	◊ Use our Voice to Threaten Vengeance, Retaliation, Retribution
◊ Describe with hope the Joyful outcome available	←	◊ Rationalize that our divisive actions were caused by them
◊ Train to produce Patience & Perseverance	←	◊ In Pride & frustration, Lie & Deceive (…for their own good)
◊ Coach to develop Self Control	←	◊ Abuse whatever Power we may think we have

I do not have or use authority over people. I do not tell people what to do. I am committed to:

- Being Taught and Trained By Jesus
- Being Led by the Holy Spirit
- Allowing the Father in me to do his Works, that I not enter into temptation and be delivered from evil.
- Attitudes consistent with the Beatitudes
- Fruit of the Spirit language & actions: Love, Joy, Peace, Patience, Kindness, Goodness, Gentleness, Perseverance, Self-Control
- Hearing out all advice and input so as to discern if it is God helping me
- Seeking out the collective wisdom God will provide me personally and us together, that we discern *his* direction.
- Relational Mutually Accountable Co-Discipleship: Supporting each other in *becoming*, as talmidim of Jesus Christ
- Director/Reconciler Co-Leadership in groups of teams and teams of groups
- Inviting & Connecting the inactive
- Facilitating Self-Selection for service

Chapter Nineteen

The Org Chart, Growth And Development

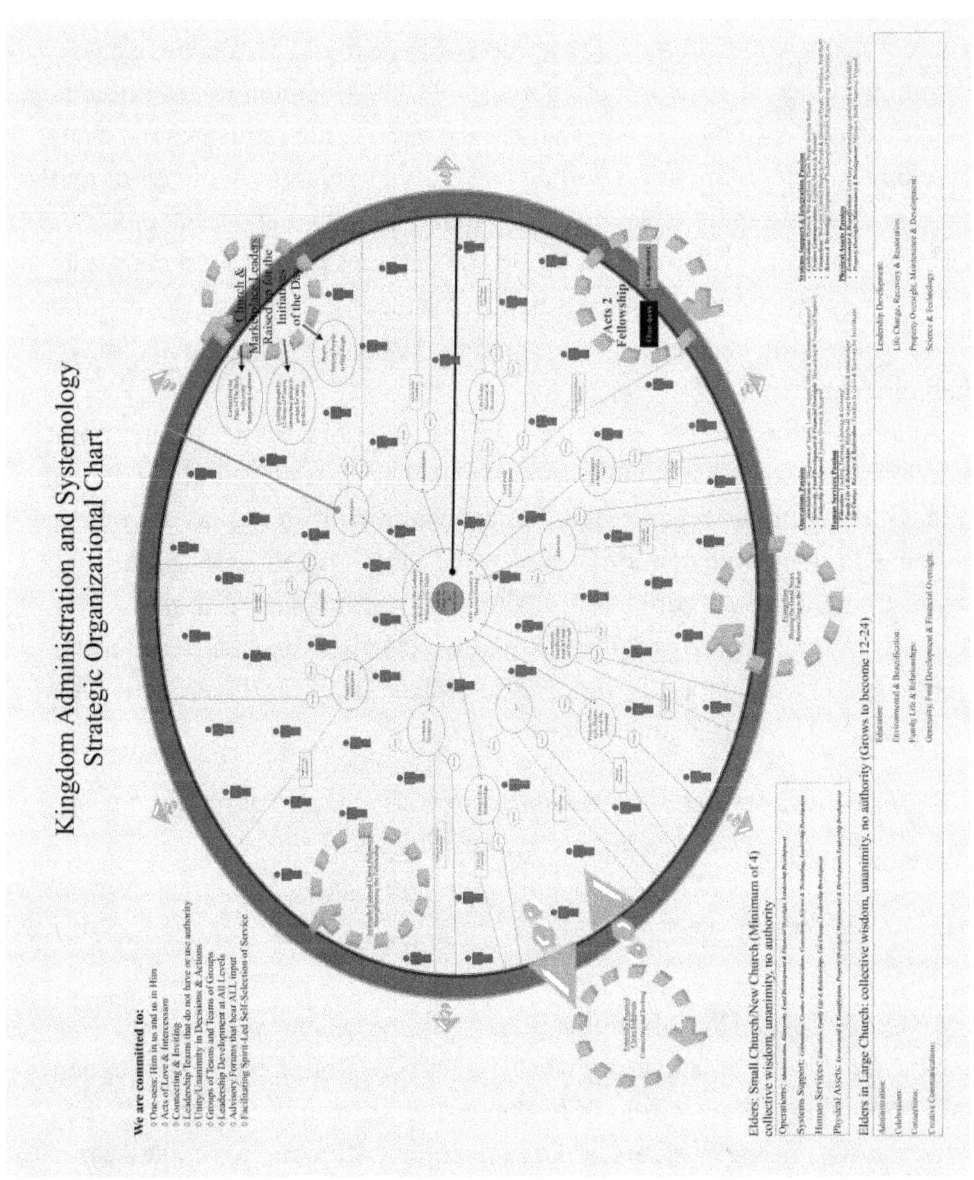

All of the charts in the *Life, Love and Leading* books are available for free download at OneKingdomWorldwide.org

While I believe *his* Org Chart has twelve, The Org Chart I propose for our use identifies thirteen. An additional one is named ????????, because it would be too arrogant of me to assume that I have it exactly right. Additionally, in practical use, I have found the thirteenth to be quite useful.

When a new initiative is being birthed, we cannot always determine where it belongs in God's administration of his Kingdom. When we are unsure, we place the new initiative in the ???????? location to have time to watch its development and see what it *becomes*. As the ministry grows and develops beyond infancy, we will be better able to identify its features and purpose. Just as a baby looks like this parent and then that parent and perhaps some other relative as it grows, its features eventually remain and are uniquely recognizable. As this happens with a new initiative, we will be able to know with certainty which of the 12 Teams it belongs to and may then move it there.

Again, whether God actually has 12 Teams or not isn't the greater point in this discussion. What is most important is that we understand the critical value of bringing the broader church into synergizing *structural* alignment utilizing a full complement of Groups and Teams. We must make the abstract tangible if we will *join him, creatively collaborating* in the Administration of *his* kingdom on earth as it is in heaven as he leads *us* to wholeness. For the poor, the widow, the orphan, the sick, the prisoner - for every need - for healthy and whole communities.

Typically, we do not have aligned structure across our churches.
No house divided against itself will stand.
Disorganized, we stand ineffective!

****

In God's Leadership Multiplication, anything *of* God will look and behave *like* God. Remembering what we learned about Leader Replication earlier, anything *of* me will look *like* me using *my* operating system. Who does your Operating System and Organizational Structure look like– is it a reflection of you? The image of God? Is there truly Unity, or is it just what you have come to accept for being as good as you are able to get as you attempt to Control people and outcomes?

If we are committed to looking more and more like Jesus, being sanctified by his teaching through the leading of the Holy Spirit and the Father who dwells in us doing his works - how well are we cooperating? Is our Operating System and Structure for The Body organized and aligned with a view of Wholeness from the beginning? Are we leading with mature alpha Christ Followers in Teams of Groups and Groups of Teams? Are we becoming more mature Triune followers in Relational Mutually Accountable Co-Discipleship and the releasing of nonpaid alpha Co-Leadership?

Or are we minimally effective, having hired small scale leaders to lead because we cannot afford (or maybe not keep up with) high capacity paid and non-paid alpha leaders? Are we avoiding Co-Discipleship with non-paid alphas because we are afraid of the transparency and vulnerability that Relational Mutually Accountable Co-Discipleship requires?

We need to look in the mirror if we will increase involvement from the 45%. Using the previously described percentages, we need only involve the remaining 3%-5% of alphas in our congregations to succeed in engaging the majority in broader Actively Implemented ministry and *more* productive service. Many do not do it because of failed experiences with alphas in the hierarchical World OS. By now, I hope you recognize that we failed with them at the foundational *World OS and Structure* level. Others have been flourishing with alphas in the Unity OS.

Unlocking Potential: For the Local Church

Let's imagine a church of 1,000 with roughly half of their Body Parts engaged and a staff of 10 full time equivalents. What if you could tap the non-paid potential of just 20% more of The Body? If you could, the Full-Time Equivalents (FTEs) would be worth $750,000 dollars in equivalent payroll. If you have a church of 5,000 – multiply by 5.

- 10 paid staff averaging $75K per year (including benefits) equals $750,000 per year and (working 40 hours per week 50 weeks per year) 20,000 hours per year.
- 200 more people (20% more of the weekly attendance) in service giving 100 hours per year (2 hours/week) equals 20,000 hours per year – a value of $750,000!

If you could bring an additional 10 FTEs through engaging more people in service what would that be worth? $750,000, yes, but it would be worth much more in terms of the lives those additional FTEs would touch and bring together. And what would that be worth in your church community? Additionally, imagine the value of eliminating Outside Services or Janitorial Payroll as The Body aligns itself in Service and Study Groups around areas of passionate interest.

Janitors for Jesus (JfJ) is a Team of Service & Study Groups committed to eliminating the cost of janitorial services and the provision of appropriate restroom conditions. *JfJ* has overarching leadership (functioning in Co-Leadership and Co-Discipleship) that facilitates the *Janitors for Jesus* small groups. They are accountable for supporting the groups and lean on each of the church's 12 Teams for Advice and Supportive Service. The church's structure of 4 Groups and 12 Teams provide *JfJ* support in the following ways:

- **Operations Group**
  - Administration Team – organization and supplies
  - Generosity, Fund Development & Financial Oversight – budgeting
  - Leadership Development Team – leader growth & support
- **Systems Support & Integration Group**
  - Celebrations Team – periodic encouragement as they serve
  - Creative Communications Team – marketing to grow *JfJ*
  - Connections Team – people identification and connection
  - Science & Technology Team – support for systems use
- **Human Services Group**
  - Education Team – study materials & teaching
  - Family Life & Relationships Team – counseling, mentoring & support
  - Life Change, Recovery & Restoration Team – Individual support
- **Physical Assets Group**
  - Environment & Beautification Team – collaboration
  - Property Oversight, Maintenance & Development Team – leader growth and support

As should all of our ministries, *Janitors for Jesus* may best be characterized as *a scaling church plant within a church*. Just as with any church plant, the initial *JfJ* Co-Leaders function as all 4 Groups and all 12 Teams. Wisdom and discernment are required to avoid activating *JfJ* with too few leaders. Minimally, in a small church setting, *JfJ* Co-Leaders are required for each of the 4 Groups (8 people), though in larger churches these must fill leadership of all 12 Teams before attempting full ministry function and activities.

At birth, two Co-Leaders look for those needed to fill out Co-Leadership of the 4 Groups. Then, the 8 look to become 12 who then look to become 24. Many hands make for light work. Jesus told us that his yolk upon us is easy and his burden upon us light!

Unlike a true church plant, the birthing of *JfJ* will receive support from all 12 Teams of the broader church. For example, the Connections Team will support the development of a *JfJ* Connections Team that will integrate with it. The same would be true for each of the other 11 Teams.

One of the ways of developing Co-Leadership for all 12 of the *JfJ* Teams is through the temporary involvement of members from the 12 Teams of the broader church. As they work with the initial *JfJ* Co-Leaders to identify a full complement of *JfJ* Team Co-Leadership, they also temporarily function *as JfJ* Team Co-leaders. Once they have been able to support the placement and establishment of the *JfJ* Co-Leader Teams, they provide ongoing *JfJ* Team integration via their roles with the Teams of the broader church.

JfJ Teams may start with as few as 4 development minded Co-Leaders who grow 12 Co-Leadership Teams such that a rotation of 7 Service and Study Groups (10-12 people each) are on duty.

As you might expect, some members are not as passionate for saving the church money as they are the quality of the attender environment. One *JfJ* member relates that it is not money or sanitation that leads him to serve. It is simply "something that I'm good at, and as a widower it avails me time with friends in a small group that meets more frequently than just a bible study – and it's action orientation helps me know that I am helping people to enjoy their church experience!"

One of the Co-Leaders - who "works" 10 hours each week with *JfJ* - said that he felt led to start the Service and Study Group when he saw a new attender walk into a restroom with her baby during church. When she suddenly came out and left, he asked a woman nearby to go in to see if everything was OK in there. He came to learn that the restroom condition was quite unsanitary. Leadership was aware of the situation, but they were having trouble securing timely janitorial services.

When he volunteered to take the lead for doing the cleaning in-house, they paired him with an unpaid and diversely gifted Co-Leader. They adopted Adonai's Unity Operating System & Structure and submitted to each other in Co-Leadership and Relational Mutually Accountable Co-Discipleship for the development of 6 more groups. Their friendship is now legendary, and their service reliable - a model for every Service and Study Group started afterwards.

What if you had *JfJ* type small groups that handled lawn and landscape, HVAC, flooring, painting, masonry care, asphalt sealing, etc., etc.? What if your goal was to facilitate passion-aligned Co-Leadership and Co-Discipleship in every ministry such that Teams of Groups and Groups of Teams organized within small group models - saving more money for *the widows and the orphans*?

The role of the leader is to equip/prepare/facilitate the people to acts of service.

Matthew 25:21
His master said to him, 'Well done, good and faithful servant. You have been faithful over a little; I will set you over much.
Enter into the joy of your master.'

Chapter Twenty

Facilitating Ministry Self-Selection

Using the 12 Teams of his Unity Operating System and Structure, we are better able to remain United, provide *facilitative vision across all Teams* for synergized collaboration and better sustain our relationships. Using it, EVERY ministry you can imagine will fit within one of the 12 Teams and every potential minister will have a better chance of finding their Connection to satisfying ministry within a committed small group, study group, service group or missional community.

When we post our vision and structure online and in our public places, high-capacity leaders have a better chance of imagining where we collectively discern we are going. This goes a long way toward facilitative Transparency and a Connective view for every Part of The Body.

Together, God given passion, giftedness and sense of call draw us to places of service. The role of the leader is to equip/prepare/facilitate the people to acts of service. Besides "Love Wholly, Love Only", we are each so unique that none of us can really know what another is called to do. Therefore, as we consider God's calling for ourselves and others, we will better Connect people when we provide a Whole Body Structure for viewing that aids them in Self-Selection.

When we value our differences and facilitate equipping and Connection for all according to their personal discernment of *God's* leading, people will less frequently *Self-Select out* and more often get in and *Self-Select to stay in.* As we contemplate uniting the Whole Body with every supporting ligament, we would do well to value the grand diversity of our individuality and the leadership of the Holy Spirit.

Internal, External, Evangelical

Huge untapped potential lies dormant within the borders of our churches and communities. Having already offered their support, transformational alpha potential is just sitting there wondering why their suggestions have fallen on deaf ears and why they have been somehow rejected. The result is that 45% of our Active Implementers are inactive.

Some percentage of them desire to be in productive service but cannot find their fit. Some are Internals unable to passionately align in ministry with you because the very alphas you need to lead them are part of the 45%! Others are Externals who can't find their way through to the non-profit options. When we put these inactive people of similar passion and differing giftedness together, we will transform our congregations and our communities. Really.

John 7:38-39

38 Whoever believes in me, as the Scripture has said, '<u>Out of his heart will flow rivers of living water</u>.'" 39 Now this he said about the Spirit, whom those who believed in him were to receive, for as yet the Spirit had not been given, because Jesus was not yet glorified.

Currently, across more than 150 communities nationally, the Spirit is leading us to partner with each other to flow such that communities are being transformed. Yours can be one of them, but far better than we do now, we need to support the many diverse personalities, passions and giftedness.

Please consider that we need Internals to help all of us graduate, *become* active and be a flow through to others. Some of these will *become* Externals and Evangelicals who will go flow outside, into our communities.

- **Internally focused followers** are people who passionately enjoy helping, participating, contributing, and making things happen for people *within* the church. (spiritual formation teams, mentoring teams, worship teams, youth ministry, greeter teams, *JfJ* teams, care teams, small groups, etc.)
- **Externally focused followers** are people who actively attend services, but whose hearts are passionate for service in the larger community *outside* of the church (homelessness, hunger, addiction, poverty, juvenile crime, teen pregnancy, etc.)
- **Evangelically focused followers** desire to reconcile people to the Father through Christ, wherever they may be. Whether *inside* or *outside* of church they stand passionately at the ready to share the hope they have (sitting in Starbucks or somewhere in church). The Evangelically focused follower is always excited to be able to Connect new believers to the Internally focused teams to support them in their

current state of need, mature them in understanding, and support them in *becoming* active.

Jesus said, "I came to heal the sick…."

- **Internals**: Church Hospital
- **Externals**: Community Hospital
- **Evangelical**: Great Commission Hospital

It is certainly possible for every person to serve in all three of these ways depending upon the environment they are in, but our preference will tend to be more for one of them than the other two. Innovative leaders have begun helping God's people to understand this environmental preference, their God given people preference and the practical application of their giftedness in service to a given Cause and/or People Group.

When the Connections Team additionally provides descriptive Service Opportunities for the needs of every new and existing Project or Program, The Issues Of The Day may be more effectively publicized and promoted. Most people are better able to Self-Select when we support them by being organized according to the People Groups, Causes and Purposes for whom or for which they have a Passionate Interest.

The Community Service and Support Network

If we will transform our communities, we need to have an *aligned* organizational vision *for our communities* that is broader than our *individual organizational* efforts. By the end of 2025, the Community Service and Support Network will be online at www.CSASNetwork.org to facilitate the birth of free volunteer Human Resource Departments that help people community-wide quickly sort through their *personalized* options so as to be able to self-select *passion-aligned involvement* with any church or non-profit.

The Community Service and Support Network site will include all that is needed for faithful founders in any city to quickly birth *their own local site* on the CSASNetwork site. Organized into the 4 Groups and 12 Teams previously described, any city of any size will be able to birth and maintain access *for free*. Everything needed to support local founders in the development of the initial 4 Groups and for expansion into the 12 Teams is being included. At the end of this book, as you read The Epilogue, I hope you will be able to imagine the great value that utilizing the Community Service and Support Network site offers.

"If the Church is genuine, it must always involve love as the most important single attribute ... a society consciously and deliberately devoted to the task of seeing how love can be made real and demonstrating love in practice. ... If God, as we believe, is truly revealed in the life of Christ, the most important thing to Him is the creation of centers of loving fellowship, which in turn infect the world. Whether the world can be redeemed in this way we do not know, but it is at least clear that there is no other way."
Elton Trueblood, The Company of the Committed
(Harper & Row, 1961), 97-98, 113.

As you read the next few chapters regarding development in a church, recognize that a similar process could be used in rolling it out to a city.

Life, Love and Leading are available free *and* as pdfs to grow individuals in their understanding of God's foundational principals – that each *become* a talmid. As talmidim grow in their understanding, they will *become* sheep who know God's voice and follow. As each are led by the power of the Holy Spirit in their life, they will be able to use the Community Service and Support Network site to find their fit and Connect into service. As they serve in relationship with others, with hearts after the Father and the mind of Christ, we and they may expect that the Spirit will lead them into what the Father would have them say and/or do in any situation. As salt is scattered in this way across our communities, every grain reflecting the light of God's love, more and more people will be led into lifesaving relationship. However, the critical first step is that our churches *become* sending churches. Not just places where people *go* each week, or as surveys indicate, only occasionally during the year.

Do you believe that God has created works for *all* of us in advance (Ephesians 2:10)? Then as you also acknowledge Ephesians 4 telling us that *"The role of the leader is to equip/prepare/facilitate the people to acts of service."*, facilitate the Connecting of *alpha leaders* according to *his* administrative System & Structure!

Considering all of our unique callings, we will better Connect people when we provide a Whole Body System & Structure that additionally aids in *Self-Selection* via a CSASNetwork site. Facilitating Connection by every supporting ligament according to their personal discernment of *God's* leading, people will less frequently *Self-Select out* and more often get *in* and Self-Select to *stay* in. Accomplish your will, O God!

Chapter Twenty-One

Development Within A Church

I have provided below one approach to introducing the Unity Operating System & Structure to a congregation, but it has analogous use within *any* entity. I suggest that you pencil in your existing teams, ministries or departments alongside the 12 Teams as you go in consideration. ALL of yours will fit under one of the 12 Teams for better scalability and development. More importantly, which of these are missing in *your* org chart? If you look at me, you can see if my body is missing a limb or a finger or if my color indicates an internal organ problem. If you look at this org chart and realize that one of the areas is missing from your organization – you are not healthy, whole and functioning optimally! If you do not know what you are missing, how can you even know to be looking for it? The chart helps us.

The Issues of the Day
Help Wanted: Everything Without Limit!

We are starting a process whereby anyone may identify a need that they feel passionate about supporting. Feel free to dream big or go small. Everything identified will be listed. We will then ask individuals to select an initiative that suits their passion, giftedness and sense of call and then will begin grouping these folks together. All of the initiatives will be charted to one of the 12 Teams organizationally and be led by paid and unpaid high-capacity Co-Leadership.

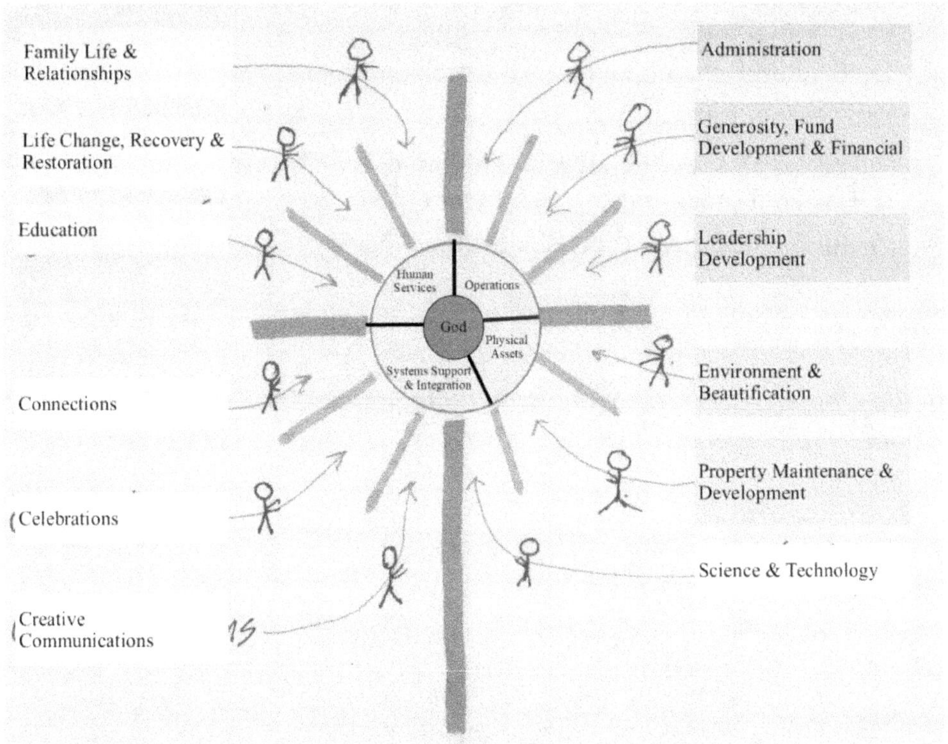

Any initiative that does not have the high-capacity Co-Leadership currently required will be placed on our Wish List (visible on our website and on the wall in our entry area) and be included in prayer as we agree with God that he provide leadership according to his will and timing.

As leaders step forward, we will facilitate them according to our Unity Values:

We are committed to:

- One-ness: Him in us and us in Him
- Acts of Love & Intercession
- Hearts after the Father in attitudes consistent with the Beatitudes: Jesus' attitudes
- Fruit of the Spirit Language & Actions
- Connecting & Inviting
- Relational Mutually Accountable Co-Discipleship
- Development of Balanced Director/Reconciler Teams in Co-Leadership
- Leadership Teams that Do Not Have or Use Hierarchy/Authority
- Unity/Unanimity in Decisions & Actions

- Groups of Teams and Teams of Groups
- Leadership Development at All Levels
- Advisory Forums at ALL levels
    - *Collective* discernment of the Input of ALL People
    - Has God brought us a Leader Out Of Nowhere, now here?
- Facilitating Spirit-Led Self-Selection of Service

We will gather together those considering Co-Leadership/Co-Discipleship and work together to determine the best way forward. As Co-Leadership of these initiatives occurs, we will facilitate support from the 4 Groups and the other 11 Teams.

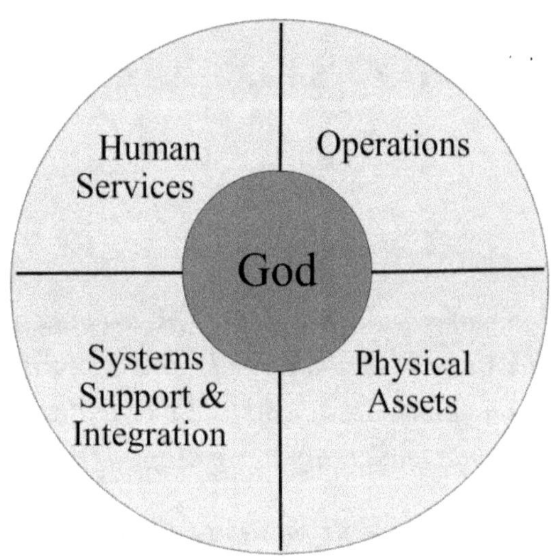

- **Operations Group**
    - Administration Team
        - Integration of Teams, Leader Support, Office & Information Systems!
    - Generosity, Fund Development & Financial Oversight Team
        - Stewardship & Financial Support!
    - Leadership Development Team
        - Leader Growth & Support!
- **Systems Support & Integration Group**
    - Celebrations Team
        - Praise & Worship God, Thank People for their Service!

- Creative Communications Team
  - Explain, Market & Promote!
- Connections Team
  - Welcome People, Connect People & Groups of People, Volunteers, Paid Staff!
- Science & Technology Team
  - Integration of Technological Systems, Engineering, Life Science, etc!

- **Human Services Group**
  - Education Team
    - Teaching, Training, Learning & Growing!
  - Family Life & Relationships Team
    - Help build strong families & relationships!
  - Life Change, Recovery & Restoration Team
    - Families in Crisis & Recovery for Individuals!
- **Physical Assets Group**
  - Environment & Beautification Team
    - Let's keep our surroundings comfortable & beautiful!
  - Property Oversight, Maintenance & Development Team
    - Maintain, Build, Improve, Expand!

****

It Works Because *He* Leads

The 4 Groups and 12 Teams will be a fit for any organization or entity, no matter how small or large. I have had the pleasure of identifying this for a large multi-national manufacturing company owned by a committed Christ Follower. This company, the one God has given him to steward, matched up easily to the 4 Groups and 12 Teams because God had flowed through he and his father to set up wholeness – and the company has been thriving for 70 years. Though the names varied, all 12 teams were not only in existence, but they were also serving and setting each other up for greater growth. They truly have *The Advantage*! The company has a great reputation in the community and among its employees, and their Human Resources Department (Connections) has a long line of desirable applicants hoping to join their Team. God is being glorified through the Unity and support *internally*, and also *externally* as their employees are reaching out and impacting their community as a whole.

Switzerland is administered through 7 Cabinet positions. For most of our recent history, the entire United States government has been administered through 12 Cabinet positions. Scale is of no consequence in an appropriately organized *administration under God.*

Scripture identifies that God has 24 Elders surrounding his throne, and that we will join him in Administering his kingdom when the new heaven and new earth arrive with the second coming of Jesus. I cannot know but I can imagine that those 24 Elders will be Co-Leading 12 Teams in his Administration. Most importantly, *in his ways* using his Unity OS, it will be *scalable to any size* in Unity.

How many Teams do you need? How many do you have? There is a huge purpose to the Supportive Service the 12 Teams provide each other. There is a wholeness and interconnectedness that synergistically integrates. There is greater Unity. There is scalability. The yolk of leadership is easy and the burden light as many hands make for light work. There is therefore greater productivity in terms of the number of lives touched as in *creative collaboration* we *participatively draw* them to the Father, *with the Father doing his works in us*, *taught* by Jesus, *led* by the Spirit.

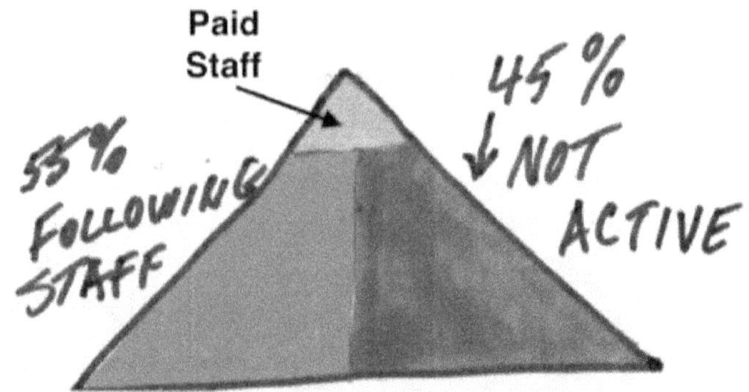

If we are truly leaders of leaders, if he has set us over much, we are the ones responsible to facilitate more engagement from the inactive 45%. If we will do this, it will necessarily require more unpaid high-capacity alphas than we are welcoming now. It will also require an all-encompassing Administrative Structure upon which we will make Connections to the whole Body of Christ, Christ as the Head.

Once the world came to believe Columbus (they would not sail off the edge of the world), people *became* willing to join some of our great discoverers on ships that explored the planet. Once people had gone to the moon and back, others believed it was worth their time to dream about space exploration and the benefits of going into space for research. Jesus said that we would do greater things than he. He said it. The One who healed the sick, gave sight to the blind, hearing to the deaf, life to the dead. What are we waiting for? BELIEF IN OUR LEADERS.

The Authoritarian World Operating System and its hierarchical structure make us cynical. How can we trust well-meaning hypocrites who make us feel cynical? The Unity Operating System & Structure includes checks and balances against the tendencies of our leaders to assume Control for greater productivity and efficiency through better *Man*agement – *Man*agement that actually leads to lesser Unity, far less synergy and ironically - to less productivity given that only *half of us* are active. Satan has had us fooled since the beginning of time.

Colossians 2:8
See to it that no one takes you captive by philosophy and empty deceit, according to human tradition (use of Authority in the Military Chain of Command), according to the elemental spirits of the world (the World OS), and not according to Christ.

Proverbs 29:18 (NIV and NKJV combined and paraphrased)
Where there is no vision, or no restraint due to lack of vision, people cast off restraint and perish; but blessed is the one who heeds wisdom's instruction.

Consensus is of primary importance in the Unity OS, but you can't optimally operate it without a balanced Whole Body Structure! Missing structure operated in Unity will always be better than missing Unity in a perfect structure, but those that have *both* synergistically outperform either alone. I am both surprised and awestruck at how simple it is to use his operating system and structure – and it's scalable to every size and shape! It seems to me that God made it simple for us so that we would have *no excuse to boast* of our success.

1 Corinthians 1:26-29
26 For consider your calling, brothers: <u>not many of you were wise according to worldly standards, not many were powerful, not many were of</u>

noble birth. 27 But God chose what is foolish in the world to shame the wise; God chose what is weak in the world to shame the strong; 28 God chose what is low and despised in the world, even things that are not, to bring to nothing things that are, 29 so that no human being might boast in the presence of God.

However, even with balanced D+R Co-Leadership, reduced productivity occurs whenever organizational structure does not prioritize ongoing Advisory Forums, new Co-Leader Development and inclusive Connections. As mentioned previously, our Lead Leaders frequently claim that these are occurring, but the sub-systems are actually under-developed. It's a little like operating a company without sales people – minimal production occurs due to a lack of sales! When each of the 12 Teams are utilized in D+R Co-Leadership, the Connections Team will continually be accomplishing the "sales" that draw people into passion-aligned relationships where Leadership Development and Advisory Forums facilitate. Connectors not only make introductions for the new, they facilitate retentions so that the involved may evolve. Through the Connections process, the inactive find their initial fit for service, and help those already in service move on to the fit that God has been leading them to next.

If leadership meetings routinely include reports from each of the 12 Teams, wholeness will always be able to be viewed through the integrating activities of the Connections Team - *with informative Advisory Forums and ongoing Leadership Development the result*. When Connections Teams are under-developed, so too will our productivity under-achieve.

Chapter Twenty-Two

Development Within A Community: Is Your Church Ready?

Remember what the HR Director of the church of 20,000 said? "Initial ministry success is always a team effort led by the Holy Spirit. The problems we run into are when leaders then begin to assume responsibility for ongoing success. As soon as that happens, we see that ministry take a nosedive." He also said, "As people begin to congratulate them and submit more frequently without question, we are subtly telling them that we credit *them* for the success and look forward to *their* greater accomplishments." We make kings of them, according to the workings of the World Operating System. "The next thing we see is that personal problems start cropping up because they are spending all of their time here."

Might this be instructive? Why is it that what we really want most from our high-capacity alphas is their alpha-sized money? Have we simply assumed all responsibility for ongoing success as mentioned above and feel justified in keeping them out of leadership? Are we sometimes concerned that another will meddle with the now scaled church plant or ministry that *we* were given to birth and grow? Is it our *pride* that keeps us from being transparent, inclusive, vulnerable and expanding? Sometimes the silence is deafening.

3 John 9-10 NIV

9 I wrote to the church, but Diotrephes, who loves to be first, will not welcome us. 10 So when I come, I will call attention to what he is doing, spreading malicious nonsense about us. Not satisfied with that, he even refuses to welcome other believers. He also stops those who want to do so and puts them out of the church.

Not satisfied with that, he refuses to welcome other believers... Sadly, there are Diotrephes among us. Most are not so bold as to put their alphas out of the church, they just keep them at arm's length and hope they don't leave. After all, if they don't leave, at least we get their alpha tithe! But that's not how we did it when we were a new church plant...

1 Corinthians 9:19-23

19 Though I am free and belong to no one, I have made myself a slave to everyone, to win as many as possible. 20 To the Jews I became like a Jew, to win the Jews. To those under the law I became like one under the law (though I myself am not under the law), so as to win those under the law. 21 To those not having the law I became like one not having the law (though I am not free from God's law but am under Christ's law), so as to win those not having the law. 22 To the weak I became weak, to win the weak. I have become all things to all people so that by all possible means I might save some. 23 I do all this for the sake of the gospel, that I may share in its blessings.

Have you ever thought about your church in terms of being all things to all people, or are you more like the church that laid off dozens during the Global Financial Crisis and said they were going to scale things back to what they could *Control*? *Leaning on your own understanding*, you cannot engage all of the alpha leadership giftedness available and juggle all of The Body parts into place, but *Adonai* can. God is multi-tasking for you – all around you – you just have to *participate* with him in making the ligamental Connections. He is infinitely able to be all things to all people. If we will allow him to scale himself up through us, us in him and him in us, rather than try to do it *for* him *leaning on our own understanding*, and under *our* own Control and Direction – we will soon be amazed at the improvements in the world around us.

If we have truly been endeavoring to make *talmidim*, teaching them to obey all he taught us – our Internals will *become active* within our church walls, our *externals* will go out and serve – *and in so doing have the opportunity to develop talmidim in our communities* – and our *Evangelicals* will have a place to send those they evangelize for *becoming* just like their rabbi.

Utilizing the Community Service and Support Network in your local community (www.CSASNetwork.org) *all* people will be able to easily find and offer their self-selected passion-aligned fit for service in a church or non-profit community – such that the Sigmoid Curve of growth in *his* kingdom be sustained.

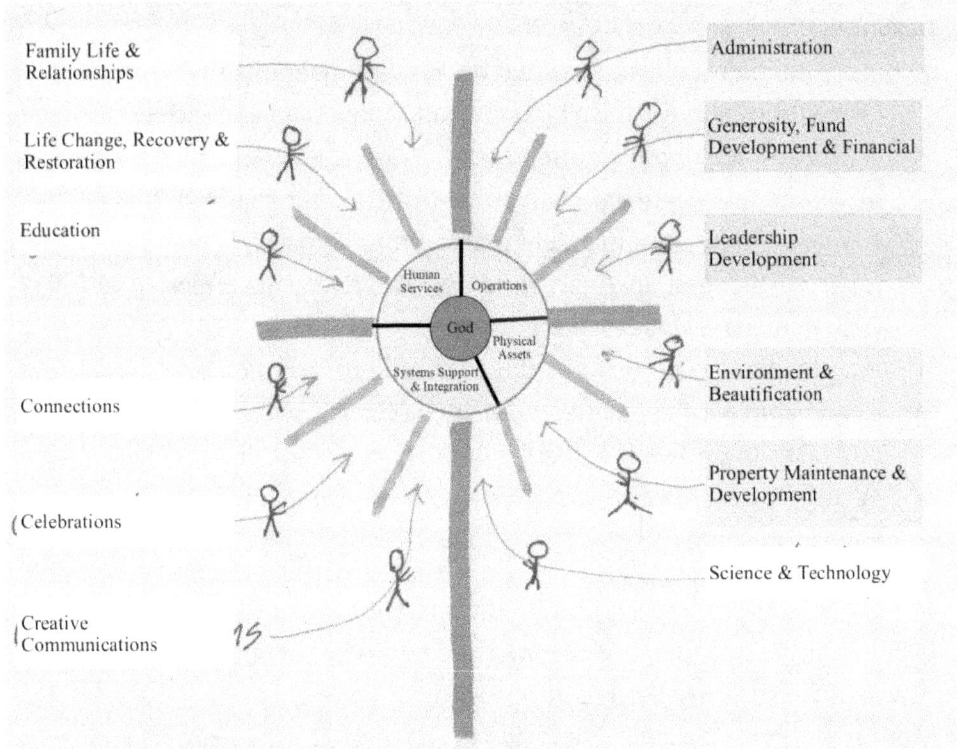

We need the involvement of more unpaid high-capacity leaders if we wish to scale to engage more supportive Active Implementers in the service *God laid out in advance for them to do*. We cannot afford the *paid staff* necessary to lead everyone in their disparate areas of passionate giftedness. We must accept our high-capacity alpha leaders for who they are and how God made them, with their own areas of passionate giftedness. It is simply a waste of talent to expect them to become Active Implementers of *our* own strategies. We should lead ours and they should lead theirs – together - *all as differing parts of the same Body*.

The dis-Connect between our high-capacity alpha leaders-of-leaders and the ministries in our churches is simply a matter of our leadership systems. Our operating systems and organizational structures create silos, foster political conflict and cause Division. Rather than synergy we have posturing. Rather than iron sharpening iron we have debate that brings winners and losers. We democratize and cause Divisive votes in the interest of expediency, rather than take the time to build consensus and strengthen relationships. Rather than gather and consider all of the information needed, we exclude a portion and "get on with it". The Enemy has been extremely effective.

In summary:

- We need them to lead the great diversity of people and the great diversity of service for which they are passionate and gifted.
- *We* make money our limiting factor. We average only 55% member involvement because we can only afford so many paid staff.
- In many cases, our alpha tent making high-capacity *leaders of leaders* (engaged only part-time) will be *at least* as effective as full time paid staff *leaders of a few*.
- Paid leadership needs to be the exception to the rule.
- Leadership for the inactive is squelched because we rely on our budgets for paid staff leaders whom we can Control.
- What if we stopped trying to Control everything and instead Co-Led and Co-Discipled?

When our leaders choose minimal transparency, we all suffer! We have all been unfairly Judged by people who seem to want to take us down, but so too it was for Jesus. Why should it be any different for us?

More importantly, as was developed in *Life* and *Love*, we are far more effective in these interactions with hearts after the Father humbly postured in the attitudes of the Beatitudes and shared in fruit of the Spirit language and actions.

In defensive posture, the World Operating System encourages partial truths protectively through policy statements and hierarchical rationalizations. Over time the sharing of partial truth becomes easier and easier. Over time, more and more is done behind closed doors where potential embarrassments precipitate further defensive rationalizations toward translucency and the opaque. Over time without transparency, we do not hear needed correction - the very voices God is sending for our benefit! There is no need to hide. He will protect our hearts, souls and minds as we risk the attacks of the Enemy, as we develop the talmidim needed in the administration of his kingdom - on earth as it is in heaven!

Ephesians 6:10-20

10 Finally, be strong in the Lord and in the strength of his might. 11 Put on the whole armor of God, that you may be able to stand against the schemes of the devil. 12 For we do not wrestle against flesh and blood, but against the rulers, against the authorities, against the cosmic powers over this present darkness, against the spiritual forces of evil in the heavenly places. 13 Therefore take up the whole armor of God, that you may be able to withstand in the evil day, and having done all, to stand firm. 14 Stand therefore, having fastened on the belt of truth, and having put on the breastplate of righteousness, 15 and, as shoes for your feet, having put on the readiness given by the gospel of peace. 16 In all circumstances take up the shield of faith, with which you can extinguish all the flaming darts of the evil one: 17 and take the helmet of salvation, and the sword of the Spirit, which is the word of God, 18 praying at all times in the Spirit, with all prayer and supplication. To that end, keep alert with all perseverance, making supplication for all the saints, 19 and also for me, that words may be given to me in opening my mouth boldly to proclaim the mystery of the gospel, 20 for which I am an ambassador in chains, that I may declare it boldly, as I ought to speak.

If we will ever Unite the people of our churches in scale for our communities, we will need to first identify the break point at which we go from church plants - that almost automatically use the Unity Operating System - towards scaled up churches adulterated by the hierarchical Authoritarian World Operating System.

When we begin to look the other way as ignoring Authoritarians try to use Control, that is when we will have begun our slide into dis-Unity.

That is the moment at which we will begin to lose synergy. Whether in *our* church or with *other* churches. Without True Unity, our house will be Divided and *become* ineffective *for* our communities. Who will reverse the trend? Because most other churches operate under Authoritarian Leadership, too.

How many individuated churches exist in your community? If yours is typical, few have Connecting ligaments for synergistic ministry with each other – even within the same denomination. We must have a view of *his* Administrative Structure if we will be able to "work the system" for the community as a whole *together* - using *his* Unity Operating System and Administrative Structure.

In my experience, Individuated Leaders say that they have no time left to Connect and Synergize with other church leaders because it is all that they can do to *Control* their *own*. Besides, some will confess, becoming a leader among leaders in a community initiative would result in working with *other* leaders that cannot be Controlled. Without the Authority and Leverage needed to Control outcomes as they see fit, it would simply be too futile to bother with!

Chapter Twenty-Three

Shared Strategy: Church AND Community

Vision Sunday should not be a report of what *the Elders* decided to do, it should instead be the result of a congregation-wide (or community-wide) discovery process of what the Collective Mind of Christ has discerned <u>we</u> should do. Unfortunately, most Directors don't want that much help. We all tend to want to have Control of the funds so that we may *grow where we know* – but we don't know what we don't know!

Psalm 127:1-2

1 Unless the Lord builds the house, those who build it labor in vain. Unless the Lord watches over the city, the watchman stays awake in vain. 2 It is in vain that you rise up early and go late to rest, eating the bread of anxious toil; for he gives to his beloved sleep.

Why block out God's people from mission visioning? How will he otherwise tell you what you do not know? Wouldn't it be better if all of the people had a chance to contribute first together? The final decision regarding the allocation of funds must ultimately come down to Unity of discernment among the leadership, but may they at least be fully informed by the *collective* mind of Christ! Sure, it takes more time in the first year, but after that it is more reasonable since we are just refining and adjusting as we go. Remembering that *time* itself is his, that *timing* belongs to the Father, and that we desire to do his will alone – the collective wisdom is required for us to know it!

****

The role of the leader is to equip/prepare/facilitate the people to acts of service. When we started our fledgling church plant, there *were* no people!!! As the founders, *we* were <u>all 4 Groups and all 12 Teams</u>! Then, we asked God to begin sending his laborers – and he did:

John 7:38-39

therefore pray earnestly to the Lord of the harvest to send out laborers into his harvest."

Luke 10:2
And he said to them, "The harvest is plentiful, but the laborers are few. Therefore pray earnestly to the Lord of the harvest to send out laborers into his harvest.

As Active Implementers in Supportive Service began to arrive, so too did high-capacity alpha Directors and Reconcilers – some mature, some immature – but it didn't matter! We knew that they were *sent by him* and so we took time to get to know them in Relational Mutually Accountable Co-Discipleship. It didn't take very long for us to identify his Co-Leaders from among them! They added to the collective wisdom the few of us had at the time and improved the depth of our understanding for development.

This happens during the start-up of any God-led organization or entity! It is critical that we add new alpha information to our collective wisdom if we will survive the Enemy attacks that are sure to come as we scale. It is non-negotiable if we will Unite as he Unites for long-term success, as has the model congregation described in the case study.

Light For The Step We Are On

In these times of overload, it is imperative to remember that we have never really had Control anyway! God knew the plans he had for us, and our success came as *willing participants* in *creative collaboration* - never by Control! Moses had an overload problem also, and our Father helped him by sending him his father-in-law. He has alphas for you, too:

Exodus 18:13-23
13 The next day Moses sat to judge the people, and the people stood around Moses from morning till evening. 14 When Moses' father-in-law saw all that he was doing for the people, he said, "What is this that you are doing for the people? Why do you sit alone, and all the people stand around you from morning till evening?" 15 And Moses said to his father-in-law, "Because the people come to me to inquire of God; 16 when they have a dispute, they come to me and I decide between one person and another, and I make them know the statutes of God and his laws." 17 Moses' father-in-law said to him, "What you are doing is not good. 18 You and the people with you will certainly wear yourselves out, for the thing is too heavy for you. You are not able to do it alone. 19 Now obey my voice; I will give you

advice, and God be with you! You shall represent the people before God and bring their cases to God, 20 and you shall warn them about the statutes and the laws, and make them know the way in which they must walk and what they must do. 21 Moreover, look for able men from all the people, men who fear God, who are trustworthy and hate a bribe, and place such men over the people as chiefs of thousands, of hundreds, of fifties, and of tens. 22 And let them judge the people at all times. Every great matter they shall bring to you, but any small matter they shall decide themselves. So it will be easier for you, and they will bear the burden with you. 23 If you do this, God will direct you, you will be able to endure, and all this people also will go to their place in peace."

Given what the totality of scripture has to say about who is the only Judge and the only Authority, and the Unity Operating System that was described in great detail in the *Life* section, I hope you have eyes that see and ears that hear that there is help all around you. Trained up in the World OS, the great majority *expect* us to use Hierarchy, Authority and all of its *World OS tools* to lead. Exhausted by it, let's give up Authority and Control and find refreshment through genuine *Life* in the Family of God.

Proverbs 3: 1-8

1 My son, do not forget my teaching, but let your heart keep my commandments, 2 for length of days and years of life and peace they will add to you. 3 Let not steadfast love and faithfulness forsake you; bind them around your neck; write them on the tablet of your heart. 4 So you will find favor and good success in the sight of God and man. 5 Trust in the Lord with all your heart, and do not lean on your own understanding. 6 In all your ways acknowledge him, and he will make straight your paths. 7 Be not wise in your own eyes; fear the Lord, and turn away from evil. 8 It will be healing to your flesh and refreshment to your bones.

Matthew 11:28-30

28 Come to me, all who labor and are heavy laden, and I will give you rest. 29 Take my yoke upon you, and learn from me, for I am gentle and lowly in heart, and you will find rest for your souls. 30 For my yoke is easy, and my burden is light."

Accept the Help and Encouragement the Father sends in Co-Leadership, but be certain to include the Relational Mutually Accountable Co-Discipleship that our Wonderful Counselor prescribes. Otherwise:

Matthew 13:14-15

14 Indeed, in their case the prophecy of Isaiah is fulfilled that says: ""You will indeed hear but never understand, and you will indeed see but never perceive." 15 For this people's heart has grown dull, and with their ears they can barely hear, and their eyes they have closed, lest they should see with their eyes and hear with their ears and understand with their heart and turn, and I would heal them.'

****

Alignment: For Our Communities

In the Epilogue, as we end this book, Hattie and Carly are found discussing the broad assistance the Community Service and Support Network *process* is providing her orphanage. If we will truly facilitate everyone to the best of our ability *internally* in the Church and *externally* in our community - we must think more broadly than our individual church and non-profit org charts. Once we have an *aligned* organizational vision *for our communities* that facilitates individuals to *passion aligned* service, our communities will truly bring health, hope and healing to the last, the lost, the least, the widow and the orphan. (See CSASNetwork.org, beginning in late 2025.)

Any vision that cannot be communicated organizationally through the Organizational Chart and Service Opportunity Descriptions (job descriptions) will not be grasped by the majority of our congregants or the people in our communities. People must be given the opportunity to use the *personal passion* and *discernment* God provides *individually* if they will find their fit.

The Community Service and Support Network *process* helps people align themselves by their area of passionate interest. This process is available for churches and non-profits of every size. As you will see in The Epilogue, the CSASNetwork.org site is facilitative in connecting people to the Co-Connectors (Volunteer "Human Resource" Department) at any given church or non-profit, and for the matching of people in appropriate Service Opportunities. Step-by-step and *passion* based, individuals may find their way into service.

As we expand our vision to recognize the necessity of inviting high capacity alphas into volunteer service, the Community Service and Support Network process also helps alphas find *their* way into aligned areas of passionate interest as supportive *board members and leaders!*

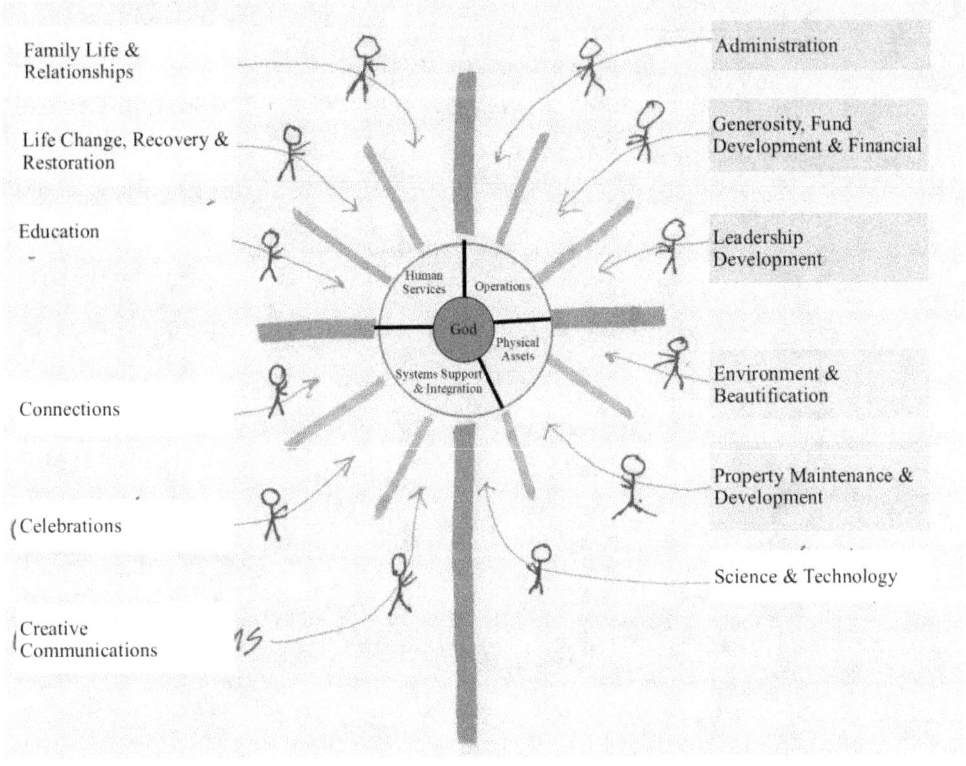

Chapter Twenty-Four

Unlocking Potential: Scaling Up For Communities

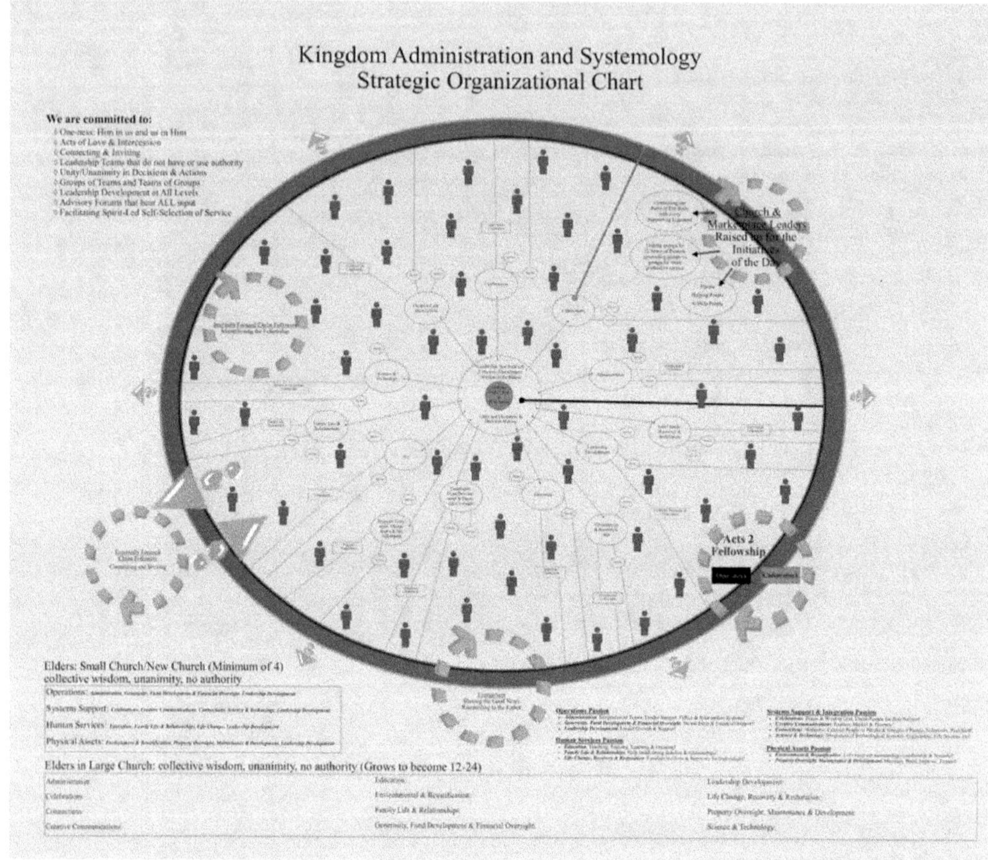

Previously, we imagined the possibilities when tapping into the potential of 20% more people in a given church. Now let's imagine a community in a region with a population of 300,000. What if you could tap the non-paid potential of just 10% of them? If you could, the Full-Time Equivalents (FTEs) would be worth tens of millions of dollars in equivalent payroll.

The average payroll of an entire city government for a community of 300,000 people may include 1500 people at an approximate cost of $75,000,000. If you could bring an additional 1500 Full-Time Equivalents (FTEs) through engaging more people in Supportive Service what would that be worth? $75,000,000, yes, but it would be worth much more in terms of the lives of the people those additional FTEs would touch. And what would that be worth in your community? Imagine the value of a reduction in crime, violence, poverty, teen pregnancies, illiteracy, unemployment and welfare. This is what the CSASNetwork.org site is all about helping you do.

- 1500 paid staff averaging $50K per year (including benefits) equals $75,000,000 per year and (working 40 hours per week 50 weeks per year) 3,000,000 hours per year.
- 30,000 more people (10% of the population) in service giving 100 hours per year (2 hours/week) equals 3,000,000 hours per year – a value of $75,000,000.

If you developed a culture in your community whereby more people gave an average of just 50 hours per year of effectively engaged service time – what would that be worth *in* your community? *To* your community? *For* your community?

If we are truly leaders of leaders, if he has set us over much, we are the ones responsible to facilitate more engagement from the inactive. If we will do this, it will necessarily require more unpaid high-capacity alphas than we are welcoming now. It will also require an all-encompassing Structure upon which we will make Connections to the whole Body of Christ, Christ as the Head.

Isaiah 43:19
Behold, I am doing a new thing; now it springs forth,
do you not perceive it?

Now, in over 150 cities across our nation, there is a new Connectedness evolving into community-wide collaborative service. The Community Service and Support Network site includes a wealth of information to assist you in supporting these city-wide collaborations. The time is now. The fields are ripe with harvest. But if we will be successful at the community scale, we had better be practicing it ourselves and introduce it in our churches first.

John 13:12-18
12 When he had washed their feet and put on his outer garments and resumed his place, he said to them, "Do you understand what I have done to you? 13 You call me Teacher and Lord, and you are right, for so I am. 14 If I then, your Lord and Teacher, have washed your feet, you also ought to wash one another's feet. 15 For I have given you an example, that you also

should do just as I have done to you. 16 Truly, truly, I say to you, a servant is not greater than his master, nor is a messenger greater than the one who sent him. 17 If you know these things, blessed are you if you do them. 18 I am not speaking of all of you; I know whom I have chosen. But the Scripture will be fulfilled, 'He who ate my bread has lifted his heel against me.'

As described in the *Life* and *Love* sections, even after having heard these words from Jesus, Judas was undeterred and continued along on the path *he* had chosen. Leaning upon his own understanding of *how he thought events would unfold,* he couldn't have been more wrong. Hoping to keep Jesus alive, Peter tried to interfere with the will of the Father believing *he* knew best.

How often we are like these two! My wife and I have moved many times over the last 40+ years and have therefore attended many churches. As it turns out, God placed us in these that we might observe and have intimate knowledge of the cause of three church splits and, in others, how his ways avoided them. In each case the splits were caused by hierarchical pastors warring against flesh and blood. In the others, which flourished without splits for four and five decades, iron continually sharpened iron in Unity and respect - without the use of hierarchy.

Matthew 12:25

Knowing their thoughts, he said to them, "Every kingdom divided against itself is laid waste, and no city or house divided against itself will stand.

****

In the earlier description of the nation's fastest growing church whose Director had to leave, a congregational meeting was then held that in part said they "would be scaling ministry back to what they could *Control*". They confessed to previously having 80% of their budget going to paid staff and acknowledged knowing of congregations operating at 30%- 40%, but they didn't know how they were doing it.

Now, many years later, they still have not returned to the Unity OS and Structure that God blessed them with initially. They continue to block the inflow of information that would inform them because their characteristic of being protectively opaque filters out the Encouragers, Disruptors and

Correctors God has been sending them. Their Parallels OS is now so deeply engrained into their *Man*agement system and culture that they no longer have *eyes that see and ears that hear.*

As the Authoritarian World OS tells us that there can only be one boss, it is a short and easy step to Advise our high-capacity alpha brothers and sisters to accept that *we* are the ones responsible, that *we* are the ones who must make it all happen and that *they* are the ones who are going to need to respect that and take a step back. We Reject what God gave them to contribute because we believe the Deception that <u>we</u> have been given the Authority, the vision and the responsibility. Seeing what we *think* we know, we try to control outcomes just as Peter and Judas did (See Chapter Six in *Life*).

We were not able to do that as a church plant. We needed everyone then (and we need everyone now). Then we were willing to incorporate them into The Body somewhere (anywhere!) because we were exhausted by our broad duties! As their differences came into view, we held respectful conversations of Mutually Accountable and Relational Co-Discipleship. We shared the necessity of Unity, if not for its own sake then for the sake of the fledgling church we were trusting God to bring through us, in us and with us. One in him, and him in us.

Later, as we felt the confidence of critical mass and the sufficiency of funding for our budgets we felt at liberty to pick and choose those with whom we would Co-Disciple in Transparency and Mutual Accountability. Unfortunately, given our lack of understanding, we Dismissed parts of The Body that were different from us, parts that brought more of the rest of the story, that would have helped lead us to learn the whole story - all of the information required for the decision. As we allowed Leader Replication to ensue, the tissue on our opposite personality preference side was refused its Connecting ligaments.

"It's a slow fade, when we give ourselves away…
Black and white will turn to gray."
Casting Crowns

How many alphas has your Parallels OS or World OS unknowingly Rejected? May I suggest that you go back to them in a spirit of relationally transparent Co-Discipleship, apologize and see what God may do to help you rebuild relationship with them? Some will be very wary and stubborn. Others will be surprised and open. Whatever their attitude, they are his - and they *were* yours – all part of the same Body. Might they return to you and see where they fit?

Our lives are built upon the Rock of our salvation, but
our relationships are frequently built upon the sand of the Deceiver.

Little David was left tending the sheep when Samuel arrived looking for the next king, and was delivering lunch when he offered to slay Goliath. *Our help comes in the name of the Lord*, but how many has he sent us who remain uninvolved due to the *Foundational Operating Errors* of our World OS, our *Fundamental Attribution Errors,* and our processes of *MANagement and Control*?

Individuated Directors and Individuated Reconcilers may be found everywhere in the conflict-ridden Authoritarian World OS. I'm thankful that his-story and Jesus' own Direction point us away from Individuated Leadership. Supportive Unified Co-Leadership is far more effective, and it is scalable to include Teams of Groups and Groups of Teams. Leadership development is a huge issue in the World Operating System because it will mostly only place people according to our ability to support them with payroll. In the Unity Operating System, there is no deficiency of passionate unpaid alpha Directors, Reconcilers and Active Implementers willing to provide Supportive Service.

As we ask him for answers to the real and possible, God responds with help. Like he did with David's potentialities at Keilah.

Our help is in the name of the Lord. The Presence of the Lord. The character and attributes of the Lord. The reputation of the Lord. We need only be sincere in our desire to have hearts fully after his. Listening and looking with eyes that see and ears that hear to follow all the days of our lives. Living by the leading and power of the Spirit, taught and trained by Jesus, the Father in us doing his works, let's ask the Spirit to lead us to only do and say what the Father has for us to do and say - producing fruit of the Spirit. Gently conforming us to his character, he will strengthen our relationships. Never telling someone else what they must do or say, we will hear all input so that in collective wisdom we be informed by the mind of Christ teaching us, his Spirit leading us - that the Father's will be done according to his Timing. As he does his works in us to administer his Kingdom.

Thank you, Father, that you resource our every need. When we think there is a lack of people, money or supplies - bring us to understand what we ourselves are missing. You are just. You do not prescribe and then not provide! Open our hearts, souls and minds to see your Direction, your Timing and your path to accomplishment. Thank you that your yoke is truly easy and your burden truly light! Thank you for the collective wisdom provided as we utilize all of the information from all of your people. Please continue to conform us to your image and transform us by the renewing of our minds. We greatly desire the coming of your kingdom on earth as it is in heaven. Thank you that you have uniquely gifted each of us to play very important roles in the meshing and bending of our wills to yours. Strengthen those who lead to follow your leading and Connect people collaboratively across all of the disciplines. Unite your people to more productive service, O God!

We are committed to Unity

- One-ness: Him in us and us in Him
- His Unity Operating System and Structure for The Body
- Personal Wholeness
- Hearts after the Father in attitudes consistent with the Beatitudes: Jesus attitudes
- Fruit of the Spirit Language & Actions
- Acts of Love & Intercession
- Connecting & Inviting
- Relational Mutually Accountable Co-Discipleship
- Development of Balanced Director/Reconciler Teams in Co-Leadership
- Leadership Teams that Do Not Have or Use Hierarchy/Authority
- Unity/Unanimity in Decisions & Actions
- Groups of Teams and Teams of Groups
- Leadership Development at All Levels
- Advisory Forums at ALL levels
    - *Collective discernment of the Input of ALL People*
    - *Has God brought us a Leader Out Of Nowhere, now here?*
- Facilitating Spirit-Led Self-Selection of Service

Identifying

- Alpha Leaders Being Raised up for the Initiatives of the Day
- Internally Focused Christ Followers Strengthening the Fellowship
- Externally Focused Christ Followers Engaged in the Community

Facilitating Spirit-Led Self-Selection of Service in The Kingdom of God

Operations Passion:

- *Administration*: Integration of Teams, Leader Support, Office & Information Systems!
- *Generosity, Fund Development & Financial Oversight*: Stewardship & Financial Support!
- *Leadership Development*: Leader Growth & Support!

Human Services Passion:

- *Education*: Teaching, Training, Learning & Growing!
- *Family Life & Relationships*: Help build strong families & relationships!
- *Life Change, Recovery & Restoration*: Families in Crisis & Recovery for Individuals!

Systems Support & Integration Passion:

- *Celebrations*: Praise & Worship God, Thank People for their Service!
- *Creative Communications*: Explain, Market & Promote!
- *Connections*: Welcome, Connect People to People & Groups of People, Volunteers, Paid Staff!
- *Science & Technology*: Integration of Technological Systems, Engineering, Life Science, etc!

Physical Assets Passion:

- *Environment & Beautification*: Let's keep our surroundings comfortable & beautiful!
- *Property Oversight, Maintenance & Development*: Maintain, Build, Improve, Expand!

Scaling Up For The Non-Profit Community

Carly (the Executive Director of a Foster Care program) and Hattie (the Executive Director of a homeless shelter) are getting together to talk about their agencies. When they ran into each other the previous week Carly realized that Hattie didn't know about the new Community Service and Support Network she had tapped into. Hattie is coming over to see what it's all about:

Hi, Hattie.

Hi, Carly.

I'm glad I brought this up to you last week, Hattie. I can't believe you dropped through the cracks on getting free help through the Community Service and Support Network. How did you not hear that this was available?

I've been so busy, I guess, that I just didn't find time for one more do-gooder idea that ended up being a waste of my time. You know how it is, you get your head down working hard to make budget, provide services and do fundraising and the next thing you know your husband is asking you when there'll be some time for him.

Ain't that the truth, at least it used to be the truth for me. This Community Service and Support Network is really working for me, and showing promise for more yet.

Cut to the chase, Carly, what has it done for you?

Well, financially speaking, we're about 18 months into using it and so far I'm getting free labor and expertise for fundraising, janitorial, lawn and landscape maintenance, snow removal, the roof will be replaced next month and the outside painted a couple of months after that. These folks have freed up my budget so that almost everything spent is now spent on the children. With respect to caring for the children, we have quite a few more people coming in to play with the youngsters, read with the grade schoolers and tutor the older ones. We even have a person with counseling and career expertise who helps them recognize what they have special giftedness for, and the older ones are being helped to see a purpose for their lives. A few others have banded together to take up the challenge of group outings: they've taken the kids to ball games, state parks, museums and historic sites.

Is there a fee associated with access to these people?

No! Hattie, they've got this process, but basically they connected me with a person who is passionate for children. She's unbelievable! I mean, she just came in and said, if you had a million dollars for paid staff what would the titles of those positions be? Then I talked with her for about 20 minutes and told her the broad strokes. She left and came back a few days later with Job Descriptions that she called Service Opportunities and read through them with me so that I could revise or add whatever I wanted. Half an hour later she was out the door and came back in a few more days with another draft. All told, she wrote Service Opportunity Descriptions for fundraising, tutors, mentors, readers, events, janitorial, outside maintenance, building repairs and Volunteer Co-Leaders to coordinate these people and their involvement.

So with all of this going on, how do you keep up with your duties as Executive Director? How do you supervise all of that?

I'm actually getting more done because this person, they call her a Connector, worked with me to add a Connector Co-Leader alongside herself. Together, they're helping our staff imagine additional Service Opportunity Descriptions. We now have two Volunteer Coordinator Co-Leaders who work with our two Connector Co-Leaders to coordinate the service. Now when we have staff meetings, we don't talk much about money and the stuff that's broken. We talk about the children and their needs. We're more attentive to them as individuals and that's what we all got into this for, the kids! I gotta say – we're all happier around here because we are doing more of what we are passionate about doing and less of what distracts us from that.

Come to think of it, the whole place is happier because the people providing free service say that they have found a way to provide their skills to a cause they're passionate about and the kids are obviously happier too cuz they're getting more of our attention.

Where do these people come from?

The whole community! The Community Service and Support Network has a website where they can easily find ways to connect their passion and giftedness to help organizations doing things for the kinds of people they care most about.

OK, I think I've heard a little about this part, but I didn't think I wanted to have to sort through all of the crazies that might find their way to me.

No, no, that doesn't happen. Your Connector Co-Leaders are the filter for those people. What it comes down to is building relationships of trust with your Connector Co-Leaders. Connectors work like the Human Resources department for volunteers – actually, I've decided to ask mine if they wouldn't mind being my Connectors for staff hires also!

OK, so how does the website draw people to you?

Here, take a look at my computer and I'll show you. The Community Service and Support Network Leadership sets up with these four Groups that break out into 12 Organizational Teams. Each of the 12 Teams help each of the other eleven Teams in Supportive Service through their area of expertise:

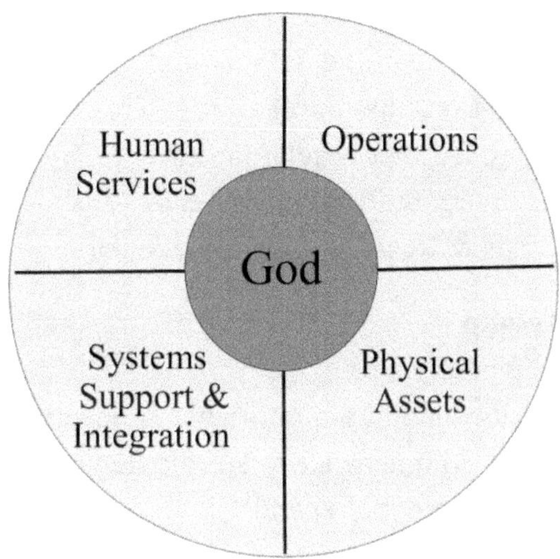

- **Operations Group**
  - Administration Team
    - Integration of Teams, Leader Support, Office & Information Systems!
  - Generosity, Fund Development & Financial Oversight Team
    - Stewardship & Financial Support!
  - Leadership Development Team
    - Leader Growth & Support!

- **Systems Support & Integration Group**
  - Celebrations Team
    - Praise & Worship God, Thank People for their Service!
  - Creative Communications Team
    - Explain, Market & Promote!
  - Connections Team
    - Welcome People, Connect People & Groups of People, Volunteers, Paid Staff!
  - Science & Technology Team
    - Integration of Technological Systems, Engineering, Life Science, etc!

- **Human Services Group**
  - Education Team
    - Teaching, Training, Learning & Growing!
  - Family Life & Relationships Team
    - Help build strong families & relationships!
  - Life Change, Recovery & Restoration Team
    - Families in Crisis & Recovery for Individuals!

- **Physical Assets Group**
  - Environment & Beautification Team
    - Let's keep our surroundings comfortable & beautiful!
  - Property Oversight, Maintenance & Development Team
    - Maintain, Build, Improve, Expand!

Interested people go to the Community Service and Support Network website and then consider helping out on a project or perhaps weekly or monthly needs. The website helps narrow down all of the available Service Opportunities in the community to just the ones that they would likely be interested in.

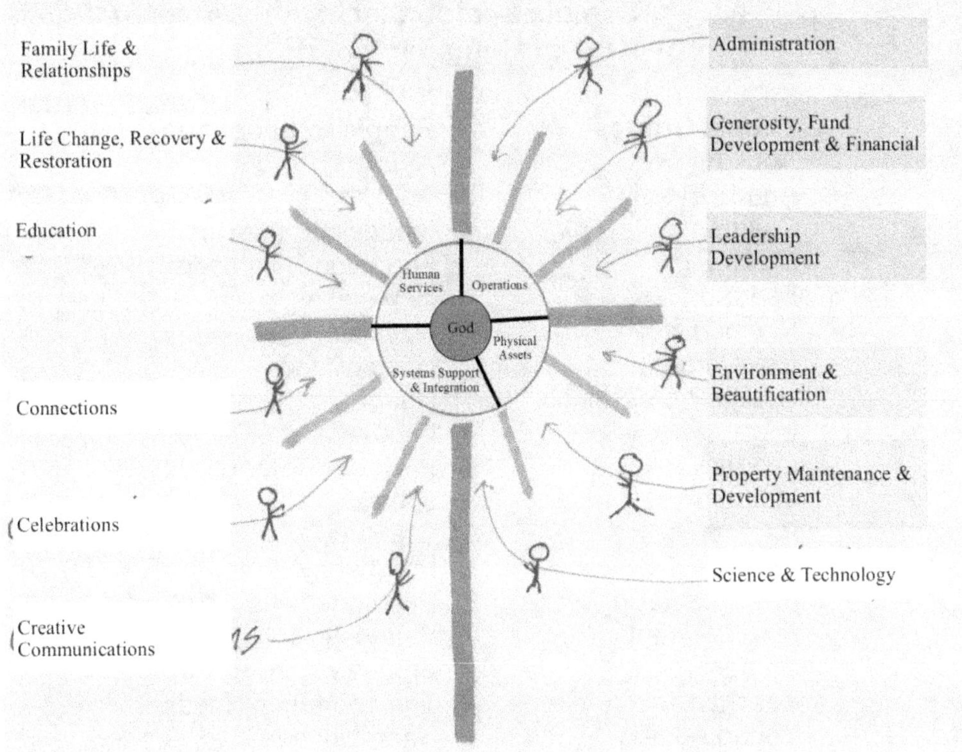

Project help is great and is an important part of getting bigger things done, like replacing our roof, but the help that really keeps the stress off comes through the regular volunteers. Six categories narrow the auto-search in real time as a person clicks a preference.

Anyone can start by selecting a *People Group* for which they have compassion. Next, they select a *Situation* that these people find themselves in. That's the key. If, for example, I would like to help the People Group "Children" in some way (and select "Children" from the list) and then am also able to imagine myself applying my compassion for kids to "Orphans" (selecting "Orphans" from the People in Situations list) this is what I see …

Sample Search List: by Area of Human Interest

People Groups

Adults
Aged / Elderly
Children
Divorced
Fathers
Fireman
Government
Health Professionals
Infants
Leaders
Mothers
Parents
Police
Prisoners (Long term)
Single Parents
Students
Teachers
Young Adults

People in Situations

Abused
Addicted
Financially Insecure
Fire, Flood, Tornado
Homeless
Hospice
Hospitalized
Hungry
Impoverished
In Court System
Jobless
Orphans
Pregnancy
Prisoners (who will re-enter)
Seriously Ill
Shut-ins
Transportation Needs
Unemployed

… the next list allows me to identify an Area of Ability that I might like to make available:

Sample Search List:
by Area of Ability

Bookkeeping
Building Maintenance
Carpentry
Celebrate People
Cement/Concrete
Dance
Demolition (abandoned houses)
Drama
Electrical
Financial Management
Fund Development
Handyman
HVAC
Hospitality
Housing: Emergency
Housing: Short Term
Housing: Mid Term
Janitorial
Landscaping
Lawn Care
Masonry
Match People with Opportunities
Mentoring
Musician
Office Work
Plumbing
Teacher's Assistant
Technology Development
Technology Maintenance
Tree Care
Tutoring (calculus)
Tutoring (economics)
Tutoring (geography)
Tutoring (geometry)
Tutoring (history)
Tutoring (life skills)
Tutoring (math)
Tutoring (reading)
Tutoring (writing)
Vocalist

Or maybe I don't want to offer a skill, but rather an item or items of some sort. In that case I wouldn't select an Area of Ability, I'd instead select from the Items To Share list. This list also shows up in the Projects Search area if I had gone at it that way instead:

Sample Search List:
by Items to Share

Blankets
Clothing: Female Child
Clothing: Male Child
Clothing: Adult Female
Clothing: Adult Male
Diapers
Emergency Supplies
Food: Canned
Food: Fresh
Food: Frozen
Household Goods
Paper Products
Pillows
School Supplies
Shoes: Female Child
Shoes: Male Child
Shoes: Adult Female
Shoes: Adult Male

As I proceed through the steps, the 300+ non-profit groups in the community are pared down to only those that match my criteria. In this case, the Non-Profit Group of Focus below would only show those with an Orphan focus. If I then select a non-profit, I will have access to the Service Opportunity Descriptions related to that non-profit.

Sample Search List:
by Non-Profit Group of Focus

Children's Home + Aid
Lydia Home Association

I may then click on a Service Opportunity to send an email to the Connector Co-Leaders for that agency to request more information. These are the same Connector Co-Leaders that loaded them into the database on behalf of their Executive Director. A Connector Co-Leader can then get back to me to answer any questions, provide more detail and maybe set up a time to meet. If we agree to get started together, the Connector makes an introduction to the Executive Director and the Volunteer Coordinator Co-Leaders.

Not that you have to, but since I decided to adapt my Org Chart to theirs, high-capacity executive type leaders can even offer their leadership expertise directly to one of my 12 Teams. I've found a couple of my Board members this way:

Sample Search List:
For High Capacity Leaders & Leader Support Teams
by the 12 Organizational Areas

- **Operations Group**
  - Administration Team
    - Integration of Teams, Leader Support, Office & Information Systems!
  - Generosity, Fund Development & Financial Oversight Team
    - Stewardship & Financial Support
  - Leadership Development Team
    - Leader Growth & Support!

- **Systems Support & Integration Group**
  - Celebrations Team
    - Praise & Worship God, Thank People for their Service!
  - Creative Communications Team
    - Explain, Market & Promote!
  - Connections Team
    - Welcome People, Connect People & Groups of People, Volunteers, Paid Staff!
  - Science & Technology Team
    - Integration of Technological Systems, Engineering, Life Science, etc!

- **Human Services Group**
  - Education Team
    - Teaching, Training, Learning & Growing!
  - Family Life & Relationships Team
    - Help build strong families & relationships!
  - Life Change, Recovery & Restoration Team
    - Families in Crisis & Recovery for Individuals!

- **Physical Assets Group**
  - Environment & Beautification Team
    - Let's keep our surroundings comfortable & beautiful!
  - Property Oversight, Maintenance & Development Team
    - Maintain, Build, Improve, Expand!

So we're really only limited by the number of people that care for any given need in the community, and since we have 300,000 in our region the odds are pretty high that someone will care for everything. *The problem has been that they didn't know how to find what we needed them for, and we didn't know what they cared about.* Since the Community Service and Support Network started this, I read that 10,000 people have found a fit somewhere in the first year. When they added up the value of that service on an hourly basis, it came to a million hours, worth more than twenty million dollars. And that's not counting all of the people who choose to do a project periodically.

OK, so that's twenty million dollars we didn't have to spend, you're getting all of that help for free and everyone is happier? How do I sign up?

I'll show you, but let me also suggest that you read the book that describes the concepts for this and lays out why you will want to start thinking about co-leadership. It's changed my way of looking at leadership.

Co-Leadership?

When we think clearly about having non-paid help, why would we want to take the responsibility to lead every area ourselves? With unpaid high-capacity co-leadership, it kind of works like a board, but better. It's a Christian concept, but it works for any organization. The author has spent 30 years refining the idea so that everyone can find a way to serve in their church or community.

This gave me a new way to work with my board and a better way to identify wholistically what we may be missing. When these come to light we ask our Connector Co-Leaders to write a Service Opportunity Description for them. Finding the people who can help us is no longer limited by the people we know in our personal networks. Now high-capacity leadership expertise and skilled professionals can find *us*, and maybe end up becoming board members. And you know what all of the studies show, when people get engaged with a non-profit they tend to give more, so not only are these folks working for free because of their passion, but they are making financial contributions, also.

The Community Service and Support Network uses this wholistic structure so as to be able to imagine the whole of the community and avoid something being left out accidentally. We're using it in our orphanage. It helped us to think of things that we never thought of before. There are different looks for org charts for different organizations, but they all work from the same concept.

Anyway, here's the basic chart, but I suggest you take my book and give it a read. They give the books and digital pdf files of it away, so I'll get a book for you and you can give me mine back later.

I will. Thanks! Now I've got to run, I have appointments all day with contractors for some repairs we need done.

You won't be needing to do that *yourself* in the future……!

To receive additional free copies please contact:
One Kingdom Worldwide
One@OneKingdomWorldwide.org

PDF files of this book may be legally shared.

Revised March 2026

Community Service and Support
Network

Service Opportunity Description

Role: Connections Co-Leader (1 of 2)

Purpose

The Connections Co-Leader facilitates the process of connecting people to passion aligned service. He/She co-leads the Connections Team (within the Systems Support & Integration Group), whose objectives are to help individuals find a service match that aligns with their personal passion and in recognition of their unique personality, giftedness, expertise, experience, and abilities. The Connections Co-Leader helps create a supportive equipping culture as people accept and experience joy-filled service that is in itself rewarding.

Co-Leadership With

Your Connections Co-Leader, the Systems Support & Integration Group, and the Co-Leaders of the Operations, Human Services and Physical Assets Groups.

Description of Duties

- Develop and co-lead a core team of individuals to facilitate the systems and programs necessary to discover, welcome, connect, invite, prepare, equip and deploy people into pleasurable service.
- Along with Operations, oversee the team which tracks recruitment, interviewing, placement, and follow-up.
- Along with Celebrations, facilitate recognition and appreciation events & activities.
- Follow up with those in service so as to facilitate next steps as they grow in an understanding of where they may next desire to serve. As appropriate, and along with Leadership Development, support interested parties in their personal growth toward a leadership role.

Time Requirements

- Twice monthly meetings with Connections Team Leaders so as to move objectives along.
- Meet as needed with individual Connections Team members to facilitate their success and satisfaction.
- Monthly meetings of the Systems Support & Integration Group.
- Monthly meeting with the Co-Leaders of the Operations, Human Services, and Physical Assets Groups.

Term

Minimum one year

Training and Resources

The Connections Co-Leaders will receive ongoing support, encouragement, and resources from each of the other 11 Teams.

Qualification, Skills, and Giftedness

- A desire to connect, encourage and counsel people toward joy-filled and rewarding service.
- Organizational and communication skills.
- Ability to motivate people.
- Outgoing and creative.

Benefits to the Co-Leader

This position provides the satisfaction of helping others grow through meaningful service; nurturing other individuals' faith and relationship with God; joy in advising people for service and spiritual growth; deepening and stretching your own personal faith while leading others to do the same.

Community Service and Support
Network

Service Opportunity Description

Role: Volunteer Coordinator Co-Leader (1 of 2)

Purpose
The Volunteer Coordinator Co-Leader co-leads the Volunteer Team, whose objectives are to coordinate individuals and/or teams of individuals, for the smooth and efficient completion of works through volunteers in passion aligned service. These utilize volunteers the Connections Team has previously identified and qualified for service in the various areas of need. The Volunteer Coordinator Co-Leader works with the Generosity & Financial Team for the funding of all volunteer work. The Volunteer Coordinator Co-Leader helps create a supportive equipping culture as people accept and experience joy-filled service that is in itself rewarding.

Co-Leadership With
Your Volunteer Coordinator Co-Leader, the Operations Group, and the Co-Leaders of the Systems Support & Integration, Human Services and Physical Assets Groups.

Description of Duties
- Develop and co-lead individuals and/or teams as necessary to deploy people into passion-aligned service.
- He/she accomplishes the works identified by the Administration Team and Operations Group.
- He/she communicates, coordinates and collaborates with all four Groups, as needed, for the smooth and efficient completion of projects and ongoing maintenance operations.
- Along with Celebrations, facilitate recognition and appreciation events & activities.
- Follow up with those in service so as to improve future planning, coordination, collaboration and the optimal completion of all services.

Time Requirements
- Meet as needed with Connections Team Leaders for to describe and support Service Opportunity Descriptions.
- Twice monthly meetings with Administration Team Leaders so as to move objectives along.
- Meet as needed with individual Administration Team Leaders to facilitate their success and satisfaction.
- Monthly meetings of the Operations Group.
- Monthly meeting with the Co-Leaders of the Systems Support & Integration, Human Services, and Physical Assets Groups.

Term
Minimum one year

Training and Resources
The Volunteer Coordinator Co-Leaders will receive ongoing support, encouragement, and resources from each of the other 11 Teams.

Qualification, Skills, and Giftedness
- A desire to support overall objectives through the efficient use of volunteer resources so as to better fund our core mission.
- Outgoing and creative with a desire to encourage people toward joy-filled and rewarding service.
- Organization skills, communication skills and the ability to motivate people.

Benefits to the Co-Leader
This position provides the satisfaction of helping others grow through meaningful service; nurturing other individuals' faith and relationship with God; joy in placing people in service and spiritual growth; deepening and stretching your own personal faith while leading others to do the same.

Kingdom Administration and Systemology
Strategic Organizational Chart

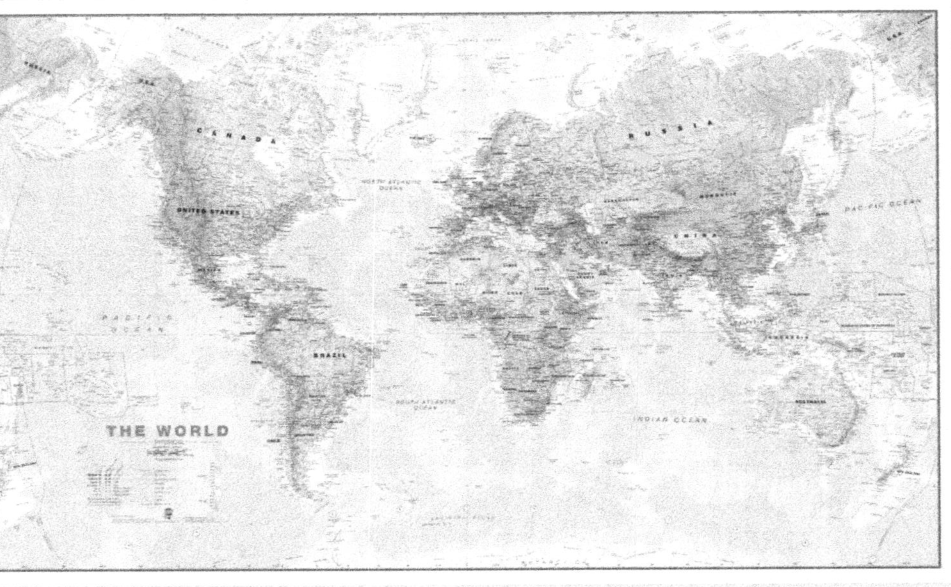

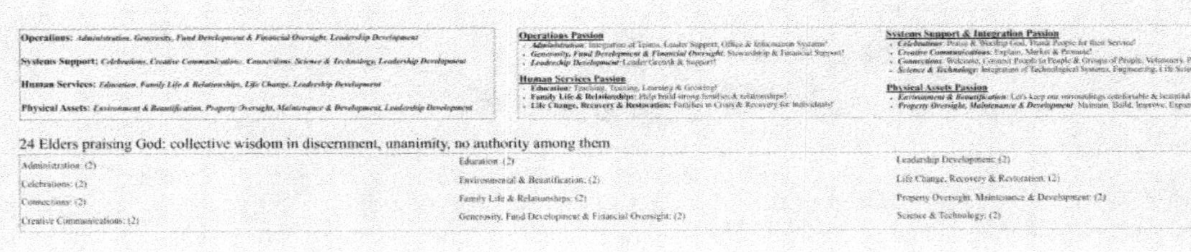

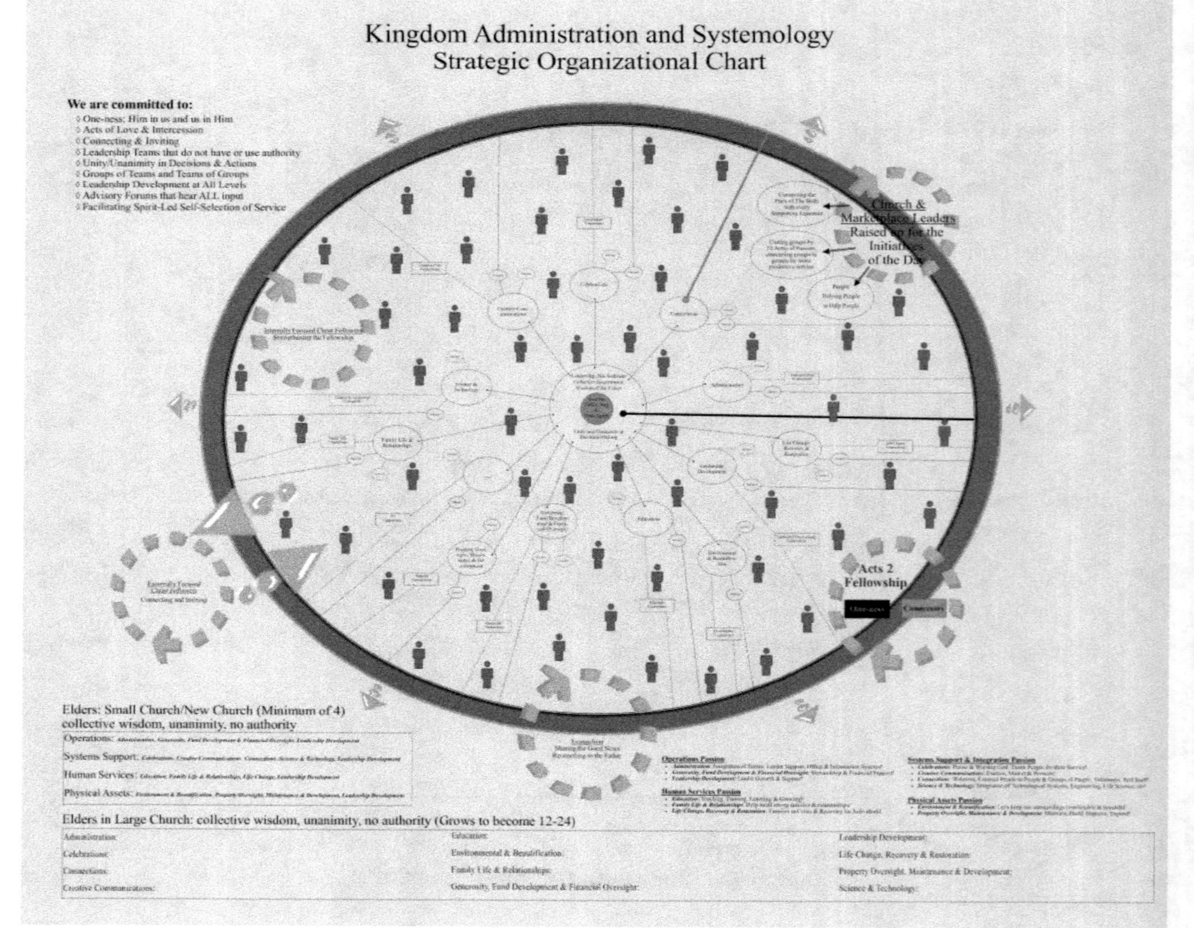

Kingdom Administration and Systemology
Strategic Organizational Chart
We are committed to:
◊ One-ness: Him in us and us in Him
◊ Acts of Love & Intercession
◊ Connecting & Inviting
◊ Leadership Teams that do not have or use authority
◊ Unity/Unanimity in Decisions & Actions
◊ Groups of Teams and Teams of Groups
◊ Leadership Development at All Levels
◊ Advisory Forums that hear ALL input
◊ Facilitating Spirit-Led Self-Selection of Service
Church & Marketplace Leaders Raised up for the Initiatives of the Day
Acts 2 Fellowship
Elders: Small Church/New Church (Minimum of 4)
collective wisdom, unanimity, no authority
Operations:
Systems Support:
Human Services:
Physical Assets:
Operations Passion
Human Services Passion
Systems Support & Integration Passion
Physical Assets Passion
Elders in Large Church: collective wisdom, unanimity, no authority (Grows to become 12-24)
Administration:
Celebrations:
Connections:
Creative Communications:
Education:
Environmental & Beautification:
Family Life & Relationships:
Generosity, Fund Development & Financial Oversight:
Leadership Development:
Life Change, Recovery & Restoration:
Property Oversight, Maintenance & Development:
Science & Technology:

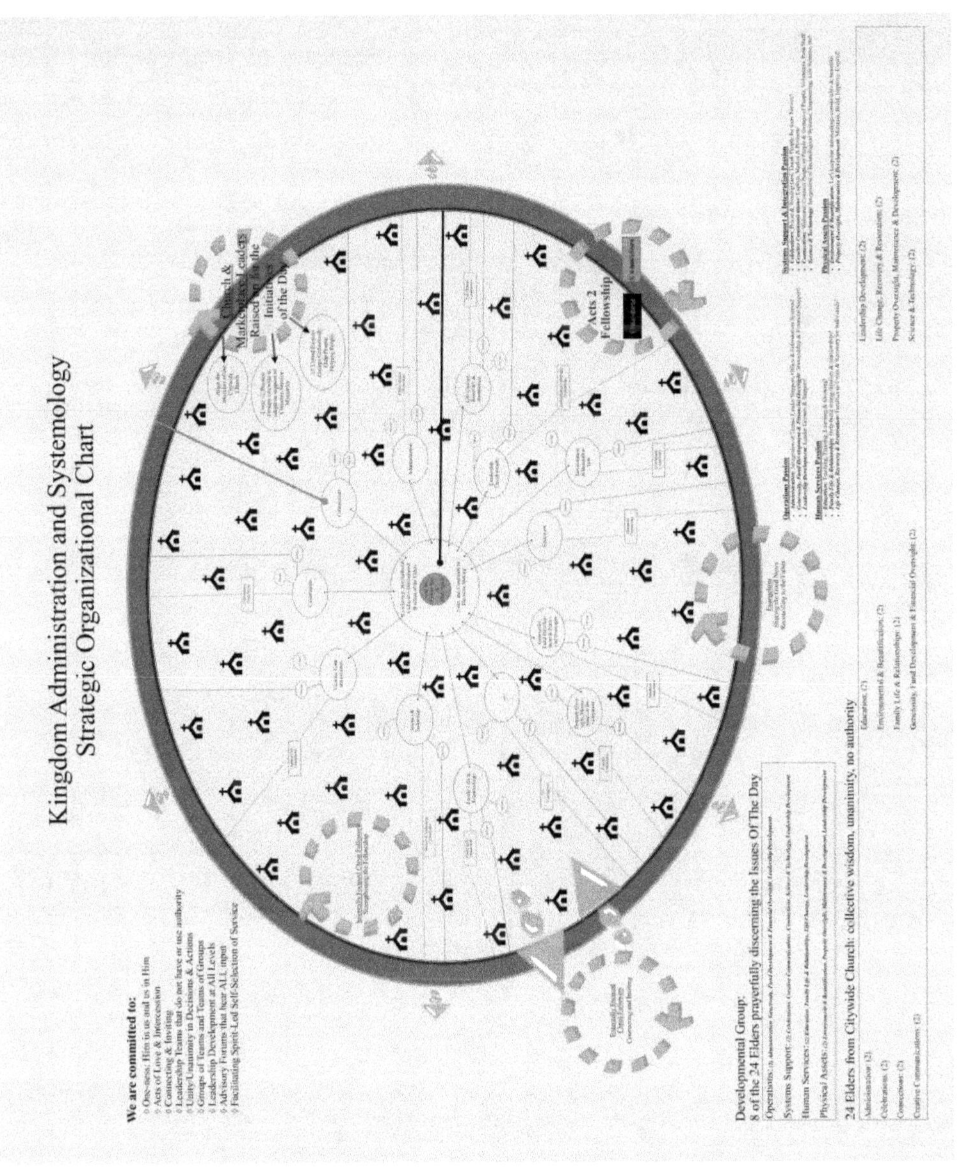

To receive additional free copies please contact:
Ricky Kroeger
One Kingdom Worldwide
One@OneKingdomWorldwide.org

PDF files of this book may be legally shared. Revised March 2026

www.ingramcontent.com/pod-product-compliance
Lightning Source LLC
LaVergne TN
LVHW020716110826
845149LV00012B/2295